An Introduction to Business Brokerage

Valuing, Listing, and Selling Businesses

An Introduction to Business Brokerage

Valuing, Listing, and Selling Businesses

C. D. Peterson

John Wiley & Sons, Inc.

New York • Chichester • Brisbane • Toronto • Singapore

This publication is designed to provide accurate and authoritative information in regard to the subject matter covered. It is sold with the understanding that the publisher is not engaged in rendering legal, accounting, or other professional services. If legal advice or other expert assistance is required, the services of a competent professional person should be sought. *From a Declaration of Principles jointly adopted by a Committee of the American Bar Association and a Committee of Publishers.*

Library of Congress Cataloging-in-Publication Data

Peterson, C. D. (Carl D.)
    An introduction to business brokerage : valuing, listing, and
selling businesses / by C. D. Peterson.
      p.   cm.
    Includes index.
    ISBN 0-471-53996-1 (alk. paper)
    1. Business enterprises, Sale of. 2. Business enterprises—
Purchasing. 3. Real estate business. I. Title.
HD1393.25.P5 1991   90-20038
658.1'6—dc20

Printed in the United States of America

91 92 10 9 8 7 6 5 4 3 2 1

Some of the material in this book is based on material from my book *How to Leave Your Job and Buy a Business of Your Own*, published by McGraw-Hill Book Company, copyright 1988. Used with permission of the publisher.

To Odessa, Wendy, Stephanie, and Chris

Preface

Entrepreneurship is on the rise. There are more than 14 million businesses in the United States today, and another million businesses are started each year—a start-up rate that is twice that of the 1960s and 1970s.

The reasons for this surge in entrepreneurship are well known:

- Cutbacks, mergers, and "downsizing" in corporate America have reduced large company employment. Ten million people have lost their jobs to cutbacks in the last five years.

- The baby boom has matured, creating a huge bulge in the population that is crowding the corporate job pyramid.

- Increased home prices have produced added equity that people can borrow and use to buy or start a business.

- Low-cost, easy-to-use personal computers and other office tools have made starting and managing a business easier.

This new wave of entrepreneurship brings with it a real opportunity for those intermediaries who can help people buy and sell businesses. The purpose of *An Introduction to Business Brokerage* is to lead the reader through all the background and steps involved. The book will cover:

- a description of the market
- what steps to follow in selling a business
- a review of business types
- how to prepare yourself—what to learn and where to find the facts
- how to focus your farming
- the listing presentation
- how to price a business
- how to market and sell a business
- how to qualify buyers financially
- how to negotiate the terms
- how to close the sale

and how to build and hold on to your list of sellers and buyers as the base of your future business.

For those in real estate, *An Introduction to Business Brokerage,* with its work sheets and references, will show you how to use the knowlege and skill you already have to establish a specialty of your own that will reward you with a lifetime of added earning power.

The opportunity for all readers is to earn income from helping sellers realize the full value of their equity and helping buyers achieve the American dream of independence and self-reliance.

C. D. PETERSON

Acknowledgments

No one writes a book alone. In this case, I received help from many people, including my family and associates. My family provided constant support and much appreciated faith. My associates in my business brokerage firm were the testing laboratory for the content. They were Bill Couch, Barry Emmert, Art Freitas, Todd Kolb, and Maureen Sperrazza. And a special thanks to Duncan Haile for his technical input.

Elizabeth Lawrence began and Mary Ellen Giles completed the huge task of word processing. Cynthia Burnham was the editorial consultant and a substantial contributor to the book in its form and appearance. Last, but not least, a very special thank-you to Michael J. Hamilton, my editor at John Wiley & Sons, Inc., for his support.

Contents

CHAPTER 1

Understanding Business Opportunities

Every year, more than 3.5 million businesses are bought and sold in the United States. The National Association of Realtors and the International Business Brokers Association have both published articles that place the size of the business opportunities market at roughly equal to the size of the residential real estate market.

WHO SELLS BUSINESSES

Many people dabble at selling small to medium-sized businesses; real estate brokers, lawyers, accountants, bankers, and consultants are among them. Some, such as business brokers and a few real estate brokers, sell businesses as a full-time profession.* In some states, the sale of businesses is regulated in much the same way as real estate, and licensing is required.

---

*Very large businesses are almost always handled by investment bankers and professional merger and acquisition specialists/buyers.

Unfortunately, the history of selling businesses is tarnished. Inexperience, incompetence, and lack of regulation have all contributed. An accountant or banker may understand financial statements but may have no skill in finding buyers. An attorney may understand how to structure a transaction but has no skill in pricing the business. And the typical real estate broker may know how to successfully bring buyers and sellers together but may have no knowledge of financing business sales.

Although in many cases these people can and have helped sell businesses successfully, the overall record is not glowing, and this has caused business owners to be apprehensive. This apprehension has led them to a well-known alternative—FSBO, "For Sale by Owner."

FOR SALE BY OWNER

A high percentage of all businesses sold are sold by the owner. Apprehension about brokers and other intermediaries is one reason owners choose to sell on their own. Another reason is the absence of brokers to do this—which presents an opportunity for you. Owners often feel that others cannot or will not truly understand their business. They worry most about a broker's ability to assess the value (set the price) of their business.

They also worry about confidentiality. Open houses, For Sale signs, and multiple listing books are not what most business owners want. They fear that news of the sale of their business may cost them customers and employees or create problems with a landlord or cause a competitor to become aggressive. But the major reason owners attempt to sell their own businesses is that they lack an understanding of what it takes to sell a business.

WHAT IT TAKES TO SELL A BUSINESS

Just because an owner is successful at running a business does not mean he or she knows the first thing about selling one. The deeply involved person is, without help, the *least* qualified person to evaluate the business objectively and present it for sale.

Selling businesses takes time. It's a rare business owner who can price the business properly, package it for sale, market it, screen buyers, sell the business, negotiate, help with financing, and handle all the legal and tax implications while continuing to run the business. A qualified intermediary—broker, agent, or consultant—can provide those services.

HOW BUSINESSES ARE SOLD

Because most people are familiar with real estate sales, the following explanation of business sales will make frequent references to and comparisons with real estate.

The process of selling a business is very similar to that for selling real estate. Most people will recognize the elements involved:

- A seller (client)
- A property, with or without real estate
- A listing agreement
- Farming and prospecting
- Marketing effort
- Networking and personal promotion
- A buyer (customer)
- Negotiations
- Financing
- A closing
- A commission

Each of these elements will be examined in detail in later chapters as well as some other familiar activities.

Despite the many similarities between selling businesses and selling real estate, some very significant differences do exist.

MOTIVES AND ATTITUDES

An area of fundamental difference involves why people sell or buy and how they feel about it. Motives for selling real estate are typically strong and straightforward—people are moving up, down, or away. The causes behind these motives may be complex, running from divorce to economic good or bad fortune, but the basic motives are usually clear and firm.

This is not the case with the sale of a business. Motives for selling businesses can be the same as those for selling real estate, but they also include retirement, other business interests, boredom or burnout, and partner problems, among many others. In addition, business owners often disguise their true motives to avoid damaging their chances of sale. A seller who says he or she is thinking about retirement may mean "I'm tired of working 80 hours a week." "Other business interests" may mean "I can't hire any help." Owners don't often volunteer that the business is in trouble or the lease is being doubled or a competitor is opening up down the street.

While homeowners often feel an attachment to a house, a business owner may personally identify with his or her business, particularly if the owner is the founder. This extremely strong emotional bond requires sensitivity from everyone, broker or buyer, who deals with the business seller.

Other attitudes frequently found in both parties toward the business sale transaction are a sense of uncertainty and a feeling of being on unsure ground. These doubts and insecurities arise because the parties have little or no experience to draw on as a frame of reference. Almost everyone has sold a house or knows people who have. People are more familiar with how houses are priced and have common sense ways of making comparisons. The same cannot be said about the sale of a business. Most people will only buy or sell one business in their lifetime, and it is difficult to compare prices. The implications of this difference between the sale of a business and the sale of real estate will be covered in Chapter 11.

PRICING

As we have already stated, the most commonly used method for pricing real estate—market comparison—is not available for pricing businesses. Chapter 3 will show how the price of a business is determined by what a business owns, what it earns, and what makes it unique. Price is also influenced by the terms of sale and the amount of seller financing.

In addition, the facts and figures needed to establish price are not always easily available. Financial records in smaller companies are often minimal and usually contrived. It's been said that some business owners keep their books to "maximize their lifestyles and minimize their taxes."

COMPLEXITY

Another obvious difference from real estate is the complexity of the business sale. Understanding the income (profit and loss) statement, the balance sheet, and the cash flow statement is a basic requirement. While the ability to interpret these statements is an additional burden on those who list and sell businesses, training is readily available, and your own accountant or the seller's accountant can help.

The sale of a business can require a much wider variety of advisors—accountants, attorneys, appraisers, bankers, and others. They all have special responsibilities to their client, but only you will have the responsibility to sell the business. You'll need to develop a working relationship with all of them and sometimes with others, such as the seller's landlord, a licensing agency, or a franchisor. Also, complex tax questions, EPA rules, and other technical issues require expert advice. Your job is not to solve these specialized problems but to recognize them and to help your clients find the help they need.

FINANCING

The difference in financing business sales versus real estate could be called a "good news/bad news" story. The good news is that most business sales are financed by the very person who initiated the sale, the seller. Down payment, length of the term, and the interest rate are all very negotiable and under the control of the seller. The bad news is that for most business sales the seller is the only basic source of financing. Buyers may have savings, equity in their homes, and several other sources of money (see Chapter 7), but these sources are typically used for the down payment. All other sources of financing will be explored, but the seller will still be the primary source.

REGULATION

The following 15 states require licenses and regulate business sales in ways similar to real estate. Others are considering licensing.

Alaska	Michigan
Arizona	Minnesota
California	Nevada
Colorado	Oregon
Florida	South Dakota
Hawaii	Washington
Idaho	Wisconsin
Kentucky	

If you are in one of these states, you can learn from your licensing board of any special requirements to handle business sales. In all other states, no license is required.

If the business sale involves the transfer of a lease or the sale of the real estate, a real estate license may be required, even in states where no license is required for business sales. Also, if you sell the stock of a business rather than the assets, you may be required to have a securities sales license. Check with your attorney.

Errors and Omissions

A standard errors and omissions insurance policy may not cover business sales. Agents have a higher exposure in business sales because they must rely on the facts and figures given by the owner—and these are not always accurate or complete. In addition, agents can also incur risk by forecasting earnings. An agent's simple statement, "You can make a lot of money in that business," could be interpreted as misleading if the buyer fails in the business after relying on that advice.

If you cannot obtain coverage for business sales, consult your attorney. There are certain procedures and disclaimer statements that can be used to minimize your exposure.

Procedures

The legal forms and procedures for listings, offers, binders, and so on are relatively standard in license states and readily available. In unregulated states, general contract law applies, and you should have an attorney insure that the forms you plan to use are valid.

The closing procedures differ from real estate. The business sale closing is far more complex than a real estate closing. Chapter 11 will present a 29-item closing checklist.

There is little co-brokerage in business sales, another difference from real estate. This means brokers sell their own listings. The very pleasant consequence of a larger commission share carries with it a larger measure of required care to avoid conflict of interest. You must become completely familiar with the issues of agency, dual agency, and buyer-broker agency (see Chapter 6).

THE INTERACTION BETWEEN BUYER AND SELLER

The buyer and the seller of real estate usually meet together to say hello when the house is shown and thank you at the closing. They have no reason to negotiate face to face, and the broker is spared the very difficult task of managing two inexperienced negotiators.

In business sales the buyer and seller almost always have to meet and negotiate. One reason is the need to convey information. Only the seller can completely answer all the detailed questions the buyer will ask about the business. Another reason involves the complexity of an offer to purchase a business. Finally, because the seller is probably going to extend terms to the buyer, he or she wants to make a personal judgment about the buyer's character.

A DIFFERENT KIND OF BUYER

The most bewildering difference between real estate and business sales is the buyer's point of view. In real estate, buyers most often have to buy and do eventually do so. Not so with the business buyer. No one ever *has* to buy a business.

Every experienced real estate broker has a few buyers who are only in the market to buy if the property is exactly what they want. In contrast, all business buyers fit that description. Instead of carrying only a few of these "call me if you find one" buyers in your files, you'll find that your entire business buyer file will fit that category. This critical difference in buyer attitudes has two implications:

1. You will work business buyers much as you do real estate sellers. You will build long-term relationships with them, keeping them well informed about the market.

2. When you do get the opportunity to sell, be prepared to have far more sales fall through. It is harder to keep a deal together when one party has no real need to buy.

Both of these implications underscore the added effort required in business sales.

MORE TIME AND EFFORT—AND POTENTIAL REWARD

Few knowledgeable people would call real estate sales an easy profession. Because business sales require more-detailed procedures and involve less-motivated buyers, they can take even more time and effort. But, as with most things, this greater effort can result in greater rewards. The added work will drive out those who are not serious and give you a strong special niche.

The added effort also results in commission rates that are higher than those for real estate. A fee of 10 percent is very common, and minimums range from $6,000 to $7,500 and up. VR Business Brokers, the largest franchised chain in the country, has suggested that its offices require a fee of 12 percent and a minimum of $10,000 for each transaction.

CHAPTER **2**

Preparing to List
and Sell Businesses

It's not difficult to acquire the knowledge and skills needed to list and sell businesses. However, it does take resourcefulness because there are few comprehensive training programs for business opportunities. The International Business Brokers Association has begun one, and some states require specialized training. This chapter will suggest several topics that you can begin to explore on your own and add to your knowledge base.

WHAT IS A BUSINESS

A *business* is an economic entity that exists to provide products, services, information, or some other good for a price to buyers, most often for a profit. Businesses can take several legal forms: a *sole proprietorship*, a *partnership*, or a *corporation*. Within these legal structures, there are some variations. The reasons for selecting one legal form over another have to do with the tax implications and the desire to limit personal liability. Table 2–1 presents the most common legal structures and shows a variety of considerations for choosing each of them.

TABLE 2–1   Legal Forms of Organization

Consideration	Sole proprietorship	Partnership		Corporation	
		General	**Limited**	**C-Corp**	**S-Corp**
Complexity of formation and operation	Simple	Relatively simple most of the time	More complex, requires written agreement and state filing	Most complex, requires state charter, election of officers, and directors, etc.	Same as C Corporation in legal operation and formation
Limits on number of owners or shareholders	One	Unlimited	Unlimited	Unlimited	Limited to 35 shareholders
Owner's personal liability for business debts and claims of litigation	Unlimited personal liability	Unlimited personal liability	Generally limited to amount of investment	Generally not liable for corporate debts, with a potential exception for federal withholding taxes	Same as C corporation
Federal income taxation of business profits	Tax paid by owner at individual rates	Tax paid by partners at individual rates	Tax paid by partners at individual rates	Tax paid by corporation at corporation rates	Tax paid by shareholders at individual rates
Deduction of business losses by owners	Yes, provided active participation by owner	Yes, but limited to amounts personally at risk and passive loan rates	Yes, but limited to amounts personally at risk and passive loan rates	No	Yes, but limited to investment in stock and loans to the corporation; also subject to passive loan rates
Taxation of dividends or other withdrawals of profits	No	No	No	Yes	Yes

TABLE 2–1   Legal Forms of Organization *(continued)*

Consideration	Sole proprietorship	Partnership — General	Partnership — Limited	Corporation — C-Corp	Corporation — S-Corp
Social Security tax on owner's earnings	13.02% up to $48,000 of earnings (with scheduled annual increases)	Same as sole proprietor	No	15.02% of shareholder/ employee earnings up to $48,000 (with scheduled annual increases); 50% paid by corporation, 50% paid by employee.	Same as C corporation for salaries
Unemploy-ment taxes	No	No	No	Yes, both federal and state generally	Yes, both federal and state generally
Availability of deductible qualified deferred compensation plans for retirement	Yes, however borrowing prohibited	Yes, however borrowing prohibited	No	Yes, including the ability to borrow	Yes, however borrowing prohibited by 5% share-holder/ employee.
Medical, disability, and group term life insurance on owners	Generally not deductible; however, 25% of medical insurance	Same as sole proprietorship	Same as sole proprietorship	Corporation deduction generally not taxable to employee under certain conditions.	Generally not deductible if paid for by a 2% or more shareholder
Available options of reporting year	Limited to calendar year	Must conform to year end of majority partners	Same as general partnership	Any 12 month period, except for personal service corporations	Must conform to year end of majority shareholders (exception provided for natural business year).

(continued)

TABLE 2–1	Legal Forms of Organization *(continued)*				
		Partnership		Corporation	
Consideration	Sole proprietorship	General	Limited	C-Corp	S-Corp
Ability to allocate income among several owners	No	Yes	Yes	No	Yes
Automobile expenses	Deductible to extent of business use; maintain records	Same as sole proprietorship	No	Same as sole proprietorship	Same as C corporation
Business meals and entertaining	Deductible to the extent of 80% of ordinary and necessary expenses of carrying on a trade or business; maintain adequate records	Same as sole proprietorship	No	Same as sole proprietorship	Same as C corporation

TYPES OF BUSINESSES

Businesses can be categorized into types based on how they earn money. Some companies that do more than one thing get categorized by industry or labeled a conglomerate. It's important to know the types of businesses and what makes them tick so that, whether listing or selling, you can speak the right language. Some of the definitions of business types are a little blurred, but the categories are generally well accepted.

MANUFACTURING

The practical definition of *manufacturing companies* is that they are companies that make things. They use labor, supplies, energy, and machinery to transform material into products. There are refinements to that definition that are worthwhile to know. A company that makes a product of its own is called a *proprietary manufacturer*. This is in contrast to a company that makes things for other companies—a *contract manufacturer*—or one that performs certain tasks on its customers' products—*a job shop*.

Manufacturing businesses are popular with many buyers. In spite of the many problems such a complex enterprise can present, there are some people, particularly corporate executives, for whom the idea of a business can only mean a manufacturing business.

DISTRIBUTION

The generally accepted description of a *distributor* is a company that buys, and often stores, large quantities of goods that it then resells in smaller quantities. The refinements here include the class of trade served. If the sales are made to the final consumer, the company is a *retail distributor*. If the sales are made to firms who resell, the company is a *wholesale distributor*, commonly called a *wholesaler*. Other terms used to describe distributors are *jobber*, *rack jobber*, and *dealer*. Each industry has its own terminology.

Distribution business appeal to buyers who imagine a nice, quiet warehouse where big loads come in one door, get marked up in price, and go out the other door as small loads. What they envision is a near-problem-free operation. The fact is, these businesses have their own headaches: competition, labor, the cost of carrying inventory, and transportation.

SERVICE

This is the fastest growing category of business. As the name implies, *service businesses* perform some service for their customers. The category is so large that subcategories are commonly used. Some subcategories identify the kind of service being provided:

- Financial services—brokerage, banking, insurance, and, of course, real estate
- Health services—hospitals, clinics, rehabilitation centers, HMOs, and rest homes

- Food services—cafeteria and airline catering are two examples
- Transportation services—trucking firms, taxi companies, and pipelines

Other subcategories identify the service's customers:

- Commercial, industrial, or consumer services—for example, a janitorial company might offer services to only one kind of customer and be called a *commercial janitorial company*.
- "To the trade"—this subcategory restricts its services to a specific nonretail business sector. A jewelry appraiser who services only jewelers and gem merchants is an example.

The buyer appeal of service companies comes from their great variety. No matter what special skill and knowledge a buyer has or how much money he or she has to invest, there is a service business that will fill the bill. The typical drawbacks are the lack of any significant barriers to the entry of competitors and the high dependency on labor.

RESTAURANTS

The definition here is obvious. In listing and selling *restaurants*, the intermediary will be concerned with such things as the physical size (seating), the percentage of liquor versus food served, the real estate purchase or lease cost, and whether or not the restaurant is a franchise.

Restaurants are important businesses to the intermediary: The market contains many sellers and buyers. Beyond their obvious appeal to someone who likes to cook or meet the public, restaurants offer other attractions. First-time buyers see them as easy to run (many successful restaurateurs had no previous experience in the business). Buyers often assume that restaurants are a source of skimmable cash and family employment. In reality, owning a restaurant often means long hours, pilferage, and labor problems.

RETAIL

Retail businesses—those that maintain a physical location and sell to the consumer—are very important to the intermediary. The sheer numbers of them, their variety, and their price range make them popular with buyers. Also, because they maintain an open location, they are easy for the intermediary to contact to solicit listings. The drawbacks of retail businesses are vulnerability to competition, dependency on labor, and sensitivity to location and lease. Long hours and pilferage are other problems.

OTHER BUSINESS CATEGORIES

Occasionally buyers will ask you to find a less common business, such as a mail order business, a communications company, or a farm. Hospitality, lodging, and entertainment businesses are popular in resort locations. Professional practices, mining, commercial fishing, and other less conventional businesses can be surprisingly easy to sell because of their unique appeal.

FRANCHISES

Considerable time will be spent examining franchises in later chapters. For now, be aware that a franchise is not a business. It is a *license* to use a franchiser's name and to offer its products or services for sale in exchange for certain fees payable to the franchiser. There are laws governing the sale of franchises. Generally, only the franchiser can sell the franchise to the initial buyer. After that, the franchisee can use intermediaries to sell the business, although these resales may be subject to some restrictions by the franchiser and are still subject to regulation.

THE STANDARD INDUSTRIAL CLASSIFICATION CODES (SIC)

To close out our examination of business types, you should review this most common system of classifying businesses. Established by the federal government and American business, the SIC codes categorize businesses into 10 divisions:

Agriculture, Forestry, and Fishing	01–09
Mining	10–14
Construction	15–17

Manufacturing	20–39
Transportation, Communication, and Public Utilities	40–49
Wholesale Trade	50–51
Retail Trade	52–59
Finance, Insurance, and Real Estate Services	60–67
Business Services	70–89
Health/Social Services and Public Administration	91–97

The SIC uses four digit code numbers to define businesses down to a quite narrow basis, for example:

- 20 Manufacturing—Food
- 202 Manufacturing—Dairy Products
- 2024 Manufacturing—Ice Cream & Frozen Desserts

When you become active in listing and selling businesses, you will find a number of uses for the SIC system, including prospecting for sellers and buyers, often called farming. A full listing of the SIC codes can be found in the reference section of your local library.

REGULATION AND LICENSING

Businesses are subject to a wide variety of regulations and licensing requirements. As an intermediary, you are not expected to be an expert in every detail of this complex topic, but you should be familiar with the categories of regulation that might be relevant to a transaction. The best way to prepare yourself is to read the condensed descriptions of these regulations that are available from the appropriate governmental department. Your own accountant and attorney may also have summaries. In particular, you need to consider the following specific areas.

REGISTRATION NUMBERS

There are two key numbers, one from the federal government and one from the state. The federal number is called an *employer identification number*. It is issued by the Department of the Treasury and is the number used with federal tax returns, withholding, FICA, and other US government programs. The state identification number, often called a *tax registration number*, is used with state programs such as sales and use tax and state income tax.

THE OCCUPATIONAL SAFETY AND HEALTH ACT (OSHA)

This set of regulations has to do with the environment of the workplace. It prescribes the procedures a company must follow to protect its employees from hazards to their health and physical safety. Manufacturing businesses are the most subject to these laws, but any business can have some activity that is covered.

THE ENVIRONMENTAL PROTECTION AGENCY (EPA)

This federal agency is responsible for establishing and enforcing regulations involving air, water and ground pollution. States also have environmental laws and agencies. These agencies can issue detailed instructions on the purchase, handling, use, and disposal of specific materials. They enforce limits on the emissions of hazardous gasses, the discharge of contaminated water, and the disposal of solid waste. Even noise and odor are covered.

Here, too, manufacturing businesses are the principal targets of regulation, but others, such as transportation companies and retail businesses that buy and resell such things as paint and garden chemicals, are covered. Gas stations are a common business category and one that is very affected by environmental laws. In this case, the big concern is the condition of the underground gasoline storage tanks. A secondary concern is the seepage into the soil and water of the gasoline and oil products associated with automobile repair.

EMPLOYEE RETIREMENT INCOME SECURITY ACT (ERISA)

This body of law is intended to regulate and protect pension programs and payments. ERISA consists of four titles:

Title I   Protection of Employee Benefit Rights
Title II   Amendments to the Internal Revenue Code

Title III   Jurisdiction of the Department of the Treasury
             and the Department of Labor
Title IV   Plan Termination

THE UNIFORM COMMERCIAL CODE (UCC)

The UCC includes the bulk sales laws, which apply to "any transfer in bulk and not in the ordinary course of the transferor's business of a major part of the materials, supplies, merchandise, or other inventory. . . ."

These laws were designed to protect creditors. For example, an unscrupulous business owner would purchase huge stocks of merchandise, furniture, fixtures, raw materials, and other goods on credit; sell the assets in total (bulk) to a buyer; and pocket the money. The creditors, left to seek payment from the new buyer, were forced to show that the new buyer knew about the fraud. The law now requires that notice be given to the creditors at least 10 days before the buyer takes possession or pays for the goods, whichever happens first. Notice is given by *the buyer* to the creditors contained in a list provided by the seller. See your attorney about the details of conforming to the bulk sales laws in your state.

SPECIAL LICENSES

Some businesses require special licenses or permits. As an intermediary, you need to ask yourself two questions:

1. Does the business need a license or permit?
2. Is the license transferable to the new buyer or must a new application be filed?

Here are some examples of businesses that require licenses:

Liquor stores
Beauty salons/barber shops
Child care facilities
Nursing facilities
Food service/processing companies

Automobile sales

Retail sales establishments

Transportation companies

Vending routes

Drug companies

Most professional practices

PREPARE BY GAINING SPECIALIZED KNOWLEDGE

You can gain most of the specialized knowledge you will need in your future career without giving up your present work. The rest of this chapter will address such topics as financial statement analysis, market definition, and planning your program—all of which can be accomplished with part-time effort.

FINANCIAL STATEMENT ANALYSIS

If learning how to analyze financial statements worries you, here are three points for you to consider:

1. The subject is *not* difficult. The techniques have been taught to countless people. Texts abound (see the Resources Literature section at the back of this book), and courses in financial statement analysis are available in evening programs at nearly every college and business school.

2. It *is* hard work to learn how to read and understand financial statements, but that effort is what will set you apart and give value to this specialty of listing and selling businesses.

3. Help is readily available. The seller, the buyer, and you all have or can engage accountants. These professionals can help with specific analyses and are often willing to provide tutoring to someone trying to become more professional.

The three basic financial statements are *(a)* the *balance sheet*; *(b)* the *income (profit and loss) statement*; and *(c)* the *source and application of funds statement*. They perform different functions and together provide a picture of the business's financial condition.

The Balance Sheet

This statement shows what the business owns *(assets)*, less what it owes *(liabilities)*, and the remaining balance *(net worth)*, according to certain rules. The balance sheet is a snapshot at one point in time. The term *balance* comes from the fact that accounting rules demand that the assets always balance (be equal to) the liabilities plus the net worth. Worksheet 10 shows a typical format for a balance sheet.

The Income (Profit and Loss) Statement

This statement summarizes the results of business activity for a specific period of time. It shows the income, costs, expenses, and taxes for the period and tallies them into the famous "bottom line." For all the emphasis on "the bottom line," you will see later how subject to manipulation this figure can be. Worksheet 9 is a more or less standard format for an income statement.

The Sources and Applications of Funds Statement

As the name implies, this statement identifies where cash came from and where it went. It shows the opening balance, details the changes, and calculates the closing balance. To the buyer who is considering the purchase of a smaller business, this information may be of more importance than any other. Worksheet 11 presents a format for a source and application of funds statement.

LEARN YOUR MARKET

You can do a lot to improve your knowledge of your market. Reading the business opportunity ads in the newspaper, visiting your Chamber of Commerce, joining networks, and meeting other brokers are just a few of the things you can do with less than full-time effort.

Newspaper Ads

Almost every newspaper has a "Business Opportunity" heading in the classified section. By reading these ads regularly, you can learn a lot about your market. You will see the kinds of businesses for sale and how they range in price. You can determine which brokers are active and who, if anyone, seems to dominate the market. Reading the ads frequently will also allow you to see how long some of the businesses stay on the market. If you plan to operate on a fairly broad scale, you should look at the business opportunity ads in the *Wall Street Journal* on Wednesdays and Thursdays.

Your Chamber of Commerce

A Chamber of Commerce can supply you with valuable data, such as the number, types, and sizes of businesses in your market. You may also be able to learn about trends in the local economy and who the key people are in business sales.

Accountants, Attorneys, and Bankers

There are many good reasons for developing relationships with these and other advisors, the main one being that they can tell you a lot about the market for selling businesses in your area. Evaluate their input carefully—some may not be as well-informed as they appear; others may not be generous with information if they perceive themselves as being in competition with you. Most, however, will give useful information, particularly about who is active in listing and selling businesses.

Business Brokers

Why not go directly to this logical source of information about the market? Not only can you learn about the market, you can learn about the business. You might even get recruited! Your Board of Realtors, the Yellow Pages, and the classified ads can provide the names of business brokers. So can the International Business Brokers Association (IBBA), Box 704, Concord, MA, 01742.

Other Sources of Market Information

The Yellow Pages can provide more insight than you might imagine. You may never have used the Yellow Pages for prospecting. You may see types of businesses you never knew were operating in your market. There are also many other directories, books on business subjects, seminars, and a myriad of business and trade magazines that can be used as sources of information.

Personal Networks

Just as in real estate, personal contact is the most powerful tool you have to help you become a successful intermediary. Consider joining and becoming active in business-oriented groups such as the Chamber of Commerce, Rotary, and your own Board of Realtors. If your market has civic and other business councils, you should investigate them as well. Finally, get to know as many business owners as you can. They are the most important people in the market equation. Listen to what they think about business sales and about the people who are involved. Learn the reputations of your (future) competition. Find out the most important thing of all—what a business owner wants from a broker.

FOCUS ON A SPECIALTY

By now, the subject of business sales probably seems very broad and a bit overwhelming. If you try to approach the field without a focus, it can be difficult to grasp. There are five ways to specialize in the market: *a)* by size; *b)* by type; *c)* by geography; *d)* by a combination of size and geography; and *e)* by special services.

Specializing by Size of Business

Your own knowledge and skills and the composition of your market will influence your choice of focus by size of business. If you are knowledgeable about large businesses and if there are enough of them in your market area, you may want to restrict your activities to these more complex, higher commission transactions. Conversely, if your background is small business (or no business) and your market is dominated by small firms, these would be your logical choice.

Specializing by Type of Business

Your experience and the market are again the influencing factors in this choice of specialization. There are brokers who travel all over the country listing and selling health spas. Several regional firms specialize in liquor stores. Others handle only restaurants. The two obvious requirements for this form of specialization are your own abilities and a sufficient number of businesses of the type you plan to work. You may decide to select two or three specialties: Restaurants, delicatessens, and liquor stores make a reasonable package, for example.

One advantage of specialization by the type of business is that you can truly become an expert, which allows you to promote yourself more easily to a narrower class of potential sellers and buyers. The principal disadvantage is the limitation you place on yourself. If your chosen area of specialty falls out of favor or becomes a very small portion of the total market, you will have fewer opportunities to list and sell.

Specializing by Geography

In some cases, you may define a geographic area in which to focus. After trimming off extremes in size and any highly specialized businesses, you are left with a town or region. Make sure your geographic area has enough business activity to justify your efforts. Examine how you can market in your area. Check out the competition.

Other Forms of Specialization

The most common form of specialization is a combination of geography and size. Within a close-by geographic area, the broker seeks all the available business. Outside the geographic bounds, the broker will handle only large businesses. This choice of specialization reflects the cost of servicing distant listings.

Specializing by Type of Service

A final form of specialization involves special services. Offering price evaluations for a fee is a common way to specialize and to earn fee income. Offering to search for businesses on behalf of buyers is another kind of specialty. This specialty not only earns fee income, it leads you to many listings, as you will see.

DECIDE ON YOUR BUSINESS ARRANGEMENT

You have five choices from which to select how you will set up to list and sell businesses:

1. Become a business specialist inside a real estate firm.
2. Join a business brokerage firm.
3. Buy a business brokerage firm.
4. Start your own company.
5. Purchase a franchise.

Set Up Inside a Real Estate Company

If you plan to practice your specialty inside a real estate firm, be sure the firm understands the implications, both the risks and rewards, as presented in Chapter 1. The legal exposure and lack of errors and omissions insurance coverage for business sales are especially critical to review. Unless the firm wants this specialty, you may not receive the support, training, or experience you will need.

If you are already licensed to sell real estate, this alternative offers the benefits of a familiar, professional environment and the opportunity to continue your real estate work. Because you would probably be somewhat unique in the firm, you would be in an excellent position to receive referrals.

Join a Business Brokerage Firm

The specialized firm can offer support systems tailored to listing and selling businesses. The routine, practices, and environment are all geared toward the business opportunity. Joining a business brokerage firm would probably mean giving up any real estate activities, although some business brokerage firms do deal in commercial and industrial real estate. With proper licenses, there is no reason a business brokerage firm couldn't deal in residential real estate. Most just choose to have a narrower focus.

Buy a Business Brokerage Firm

If you already have the skills, experience, and funds for this approach, you need only the commitment. However, buying a business means you will not be able to shift back to real estate easily if you decide you prefer to do so. The responsibilities and rewards of having your own business are a joy to some and a burden to others. Either way, this choice is difficult to undo.

Start Your Own Company

This arrangement has its own pluses and minuses. You can start a business brokerage company inexpensively with no more than a name, a telephone number, and the appropriate licenses, if any. However, it may take many months before you earn any income. You can do things your own way, and all the benefits are yours. Of course, all the risk is yours, too. If you are inexperienced in business ownership, do some additional preparation before choosing this alternative. Chapter 8, "Starting a Business," adapted with permission from *How to Leave Your Job and Buy a Business of Your Own*, presents some ideas to those considering a start-up.*

Franchises

There are business brokerage franchises available in some areas that may be purchased new or as resales. The pluses and minuses of franchises will be examined in Chapter 10. For now, just know that this variation of business ownership does exist in some markets.

---

*C.D. Peterson, *How to Leave Your Job and Buy a Business of Your Own* (New York: McGraw-Hill, 1988).

3

Valuing and Pricing Businesses

The price your seller will eventually receive for his or her business will depend on its value and affordability to a buyer. Each of these terms deserves from explanation:

- *Value* is what something is worth. It may be an objective measure against something similar with a known value or it can be a subjective feeling of worth.

- *Price* is what a buyer pays for something. The distinction between value and price becomes clear when you recognize how many times people have paid more or less than something was worth.

- *Affordability* is what a buyer is capable of paying. You may value the business at a level that matches a buyer's idea of a fair price. But if the buyer can't afford to pay it, all your efforts to attract and interest that buyer are wasted.

This chapter will explore how these three factors work together. Valuing and pricing businesses is not an exact science. There are a great many factors that go into business evaluation, many of them subjective. Table 3–1 lists over 40 variables that can affect price. These variables can be weighted and combined in an almost infinite number of ways to produce an infinite number of prices.

TABLE 3–1	Variables Affecting Valuation	
	Asset value	Ability to influence prices
	Company history	Ability to influence customers
	Company reputation	Barriers to entry
	Growth	Borrowing capacity
	Projected growth	Operating performance and ratios
	Cash flow	Special licenses, patents, franchises
	Projected cash flow	Physical appearance
	Management competency	Condition of books and records
	Employee competency	Economic outlook
	Production	Political outlook
	Cost competitiveness	Market share
	Technology	Tax considerations
	Comparable businesses	Alternative opportunities
	Legal situation or encumbrances	Affordability
	Quality and competitiveness of products/services	Potential
	Ease to run	Working conditions
	Desirability of the industry	Real estate/lease situation
	Location	Intangibles
	Risk of return of investment	Goodwill
	Risk of return on investment	Vulnerability
	Ability to influence cost	Superiority

Any or all of these variables may have an influence at some time. Other variables, such as terms of sale and supply and demand, are treated separately because they directly affect the price of the business, not its value.

PROBLEMS IN VALUING AND PRICING

The large number of variables involved is only one of several problems encountered in evaluating a business for sale. The *lack of objectivity* mentioned previously is another. Many *special business situations* require unique approaches. One difficulty arises at the very beginning of an evaluation.

There are over a dozen values that can be placed on a given business. The first issue is to select the right one, and doing so depends on the *reason for the evaluation*.

THE REASON FOR THE EVALUATION

The first step is to make clear the reason for the evaluation. Here is a partial list of values for a business:

- Insurable value
- Book value
- Liquidation value
- Fair market/stock market value
- Replacement value
- Reproduction value
- Asset value
- Discounted future earnings value
- Capitalized earnings value
- Goodwill value
- Going concern value
- Cost savings value
- Expected value
- Conditional value

Each of these values, and others as well, is appropriate for certain kinds of evaluations. The reason for the evaluation determines which measure will be used. For example, if the purpose of the evaluation is to purchase proper insurance coverage, the value developed will be based on the cost of replacing the assets. If the purpose is to borrow money, asset values will be key because banks will be interested in collateral. Our reason for evaluating the business is to establish a selling price. Selling price is based on what the business *owns*, what it *earns*, and what makes it *unique*, and so it's possible that all these values will be important to us.

LACK OF OBJECTIVITY

This significant problem is caused by the lack of objective measures for so many of the variables. Projections are estimates. Assessments of employees are never precise. Risk is subjective. Even the appraisal of assets can produce wide variations. And who can measure goodwill or the political outlook?

One method of valuation not available to you as a business broker is *comparison*—evaluating one business against others. This is the most common way of determining the price of residential real estate where the recent selling prices on nearly identical houses in similar locations are known. Businesses are not similar enough to be compared, and the selling prices are not published as they are for real property.

The buyer and the seller both have very different, and very subjective, *viewpoints*. The seller's idea of the value of the business is built on intimate knowledge that has developed over time. The buyer will be working with what amounts to a set of snapshots that you or others have provided. No matter what valuation methods you use or how certain you are of a company's worth, you will have to look at the company from the buyer's viewpoint. It's the buyer who will need convincing, not you.

SPECIAL BUSINESS SITUATIONS

This problem of valuing and pricing businesses arises because there are certain special cases for which there are special rules. For example, new businesses are typically valued by comparing them to the alternative of starting a similar business. High technology companies may require a separate evaluation of the technology employed. Evaluators are particularly interested in the level of development of the technology. How much or how little research and development are left will affect value. They are also interested in the vulnerability of the technology. Is it in danger of becoming outdated or likely to suffer from a shortage of available specialized labor? Most important are the applications for the technology. It is in the applications that the technology has its value.

Another example of a special case is professional practices (medicine, accounting, etc.), which are usually valued on the basis of value per patient or client. They are priced and sold with terms contingent on some continuation of the patient/client base. A fourth case involves cost savings value. When one business buys another, particularly if the result is a merger, the effect may be substantial cost savings due to eliminating duplication, optimizing resources, and reducing price competition. These values would be *in addition* to those intrinsic to the business otherwise.

THE IMPACT OF PRICE ON SELLING THE BUSINESS

The emphasis given to pricing in this book is based on the importance of price in selling the business. Poorly established values and prices for businesses are major causes for the difficulty of and high failure rate in selling businesses. A price that is too low can cost the seller money. A price that is too high can cost the sale of the company.

Price has another impact on the selling process. Because price can't be verified, the two parties may continue to worry that they are making a bad bargain. This worry can infect all parts of the negotiations.

ESTABLISHING VALUE

Valuing businesses is done by methods ranging from crude rules of thumb to exotic and intricate mathematical models. Older texts on pricing and brokers from past generations used to quote such rules of thumb as

"Restaurants sell for 10 times a month's sales."

or

"A machine shop should be priced at asset value plus one year's cash flow."

The fact that the restaurant may or may not have been profitable would have been overlooked by such a rule. A machine shop convulsed with labor problems would have been given a very misleading price by this rule. All rules of thumb have these flaws of inadequacy. At the other extreme are the intricate mathematical models, in which we encounter the problem of subjectivity being masqueraded as fact. We have a tendency to believe that because something is computerized and printed on green and white striped paper that it is accurate. Most of these computerized pricing models require you to make assumptions about growth or to evaluate such things as risk or location or the quality of the company's organization. Some predictions about interest rates or discount rates are usually a part of these models. These very subjective variables have a substantial impact on the computerized price. In other words, the use of the model doesn't remove the subjectivity, it just hides it.

Walking through all the steps of evaluating and pricing a business can be disorienting, much like missing the forest for the trees. To help you avoid feeling lost, here is a map of the rest of the chapter:

1. We will begin by finding the value of a business. Next we will convert that value into price using several pricing models. We'll review some tests that buyers use to evaluate price. (Figure 3–1 will summarize the pricing models and tests.) Then we will pull together all of our work on evaluation and pricing in a case study.

2. The second part of the chapter deals with determining what the buyer can afford. Contrary to what some sellers believe, what the buyer can afford will be shown to depend to some measure on the seller.

Worksheet 1 at the end of this chapter will help you value and then price the business.

The following organizations have members who specialize in valuing businesses:

The Institute of Business Appraisers, Inc.
P. O. Box 1447
Boynton Beach, FL 33435

The Business Valuation Committee of the American Society of
    Appraisers
Publishers of *Business Valuation Review*
P. O. Box 24222
Denver, CO 80224

Many groups and individual offer to do business valuations. Some may have other motives, such as obtaining the right to sell a business or gaining a consulting contract to prepare a business for sale. Individual appraisers specializing in machinery, professional practices, real estate, and other classifications can be found in most Yellow Pages. In addition, many books have been published on the subject of appraisal and valuation of businesses (see the Resources Literature section at the back of this book).

The degree and depth of your evaluation will depend on how much you feel you need. If you are selling a large company with substantial assets and real estate, you may need professional appraisals and evaluations. The sale of a small service or retail company may require no more than a common-sense idea of value. Whether your evaluation is highly detailed or very basic, it involves three elements:

1. **Price based on assets**

   Uses: Used most often as a minimum price because a business should be worth at least the value of its assets. Exceptions might occur when a company is losing money.

   Steps: Determine the market value of the assets being sold. Deduct the value of any liabilities being assumed by the buyer.

2. **Price based on cash flow**

   Uses: Used when a business has few assets. The buyer is buying the stream of cash flow. The buyer bases the price on the return on investment the cash flow represents.

   Steps: Adjust the profit-and-loss statement to reflect the true expenses of the business. Calculate the owner's adjusted cash flow. Decide, based on risk and desirability, the desired rate of return (the cap rate). Divide the cash flow by the cap rate.

3. **Price based on the integrated method**

   Uses: Used when a company has both assets and cash flow. This method accounts for the value of the assets and then capitalizes the cash flow, but only after reducing the cash flow by the cost of carrying the assets.

   Steps: Determine the market value of the assets. Multiply the value of the assets by the interest rate the company pays to borrow money to get the cost of carrying the assets. Adjust the profit-and-loss statement to reflect the true expenses of the business. Calculate the owner's adjusted cash flow. Subtract the cost of carrying the assets to get the excess earnings. Decide, based on risk and desirability, the desired rate of return (the cap rate). Divide the excess earnings by the cap rate to get the value of the excess earnings. Add the value of the excess earnings to the value of the assets and subtract the value of any liabilities being assumed by the buyer.

Figure 3–1. Overview of Pricing Methods and Tests   *(continued)*

Figure 3–1 (continued)

4. **Price based on duplication cost**

   Uses: Used to compare the buyer's alternative to starting a business.

   Steps: Determine the market value of the assets and the cost to install them. Estimate the number of years it will take for the new business to reach the level of profitability of the business for sale. (Remember that the existing business may be competition for the new business.) For each of those years, compute the cash requirements, the profits and losses from the business, the lost wages of the owner, and the interest that could have been earned on any investment.

5. **Price based on net present value of future earnings**

   Uses: Used as a method to sell the value of a projected future stream of earnings at a discount. Used mainly with larger, well-documented companies for which the future is somewhat more predictable.

   Steps: Adjust profit-and-loss statement to reflect the true expenses of the business. Calculate the adjusted actual cash flow. Based on supportable plans, project financial statements for 5 years. Determine cumulative cash flow for the 5 years and discount it to establish the net present value.

6. **Alternative investment test**

   Uses: Used to compare the returns from buying the business with the returns from a safe alternative.

   Steps: Adjust the profit-and-loss statement to reflect the true expenses of the business. Calculate the adjusted owner's cash flow. Divide the cash flow by the purchase price to get the return on investment. (If the purchase price is being paid over several years, do a calculation for all the years cumulatively.) Compare this return from the business with the return from safe alternative investments. Compare the salary and benefits the business will provide to the salary and benefits that the buyer could earn at a job. Note that risk of capital gain or loss is ignored.

Figure 3–1 *(continued)*

> **7. Testing the purchase for reasonableness**
>
> Uses: Used to test whether the business earns enough in cash flow to support its purchase price. It is a test of affordability.
>
> Steps: Adjust the profit-and-loss statement to reflect the true expenses of the business. Calculate the adjusted owner's cash flow. Deduct repayment of debt and interest. Deduct any required reinvestment. Deduct an amount equal to the reasonable return the buyer would have earned on the down payment (cash) invested in the business. Provide for a reasonable salary for the buyer's work in the business if not already provided in the true expenses. Provide a safety margin.

1. What a business owns—usually found on the balance sheet
2. What a business earns—the profit/cash flow
3. What makes the business unique—the degree of risk and desirability.

Each of these elements has a value, and the three can be combined in some very surprising ways. Here is one example:

A company with a factory full of equipment is making something the market no longer wants, and the cost of retooling is prohibitive. It has $10 million in sales, but it had to cut price to get the volume, and it lost $1 million last year. So far we have a company with lots of assets and $10 million in sales, but the assets are outdated and the cash flow from the sales is negative. If, however, the company is your only competitor, its value to you could be very high.

An example of the reverse combination might be the gas station that has few assets and rather modest sales but earns its owner over $250,000 a year because it is the only station on the road between two distant towns. Unfortunately, a new super highway that will connect the two towns is being built 3 miles east of the present road. Once it is completed, there will be no traffic for this station.

There are two points to these examples:

1. Relying on just the quantitative value of each element can be misleading.
2. Relying on less than all the elements can be misleading.

While it would take extensive formal training to make you a professional appraiser, the following material should provide you with useful knowledge of the concepts of value and price. As a reminder, the case study at the end of the chapter integrates all the ideas.

WHAT A BUSINESS OWNS

The balance sheet is a useful indicator of value, but it does not automatically indicate the value or price of the business. Assets are generally stated at historic cost less allowances for depreciation, not at current value. Replacement values may be higher or lower than the stated values.

Table 3–2 demonstrates the limitations of the balance sheet by comparing two companies, A and B.

TABLE 3–2	Comparison of Company A and Company B		
		Company A	Company B
Cash		$20,000	$15,000
Accounts receivable		85,000	40,000
Inventory		100,000	65,000
Total current assets		$205,000	$120,000
Property, plant, and equipment		600,000	750,000
Less depreciation		(100,000)	(500,000)
Net fixed assets		$500,000	$250,000
Total assets		705,000	370,000
Accounts payable		$65,000	$60,000
Short-term note		50,000	40,000
Total current liabilities		$115,000	$100,000
Long-term debt		290,000	170,000
Total liabilities		405,000	270,000
Simple net worth		$300,000	$100,000

Company A seems a much stronger and more valuable company until we apply the two tests that are important to the buyer:

1. *What are the assets really worth at fair market value?* The buyer, lender, or investor is really interested in the market value of the assets. Cash, accounts receivable, inventory, and other current assets are relatively easy to test for market value. The fixed assets, however, are not.

In our example, Company A rents its facility and has all new equipment that could be sold to others for about what is shown on the balance sheet. The market value of Company A's fixed assets is close to the depreciated book value shown on the balance sheet. Company B, on the other hand, has older equipment that has been depreciated, and it owns its own factory. The equipment has been well maintained and is worth more than its depreciated value. More importantly, Company B's real estate, which is on the books for the original cost of the land plus the depreciated cost of the building, is in a high-value area and is worth $2 million at today's market price.

The point to remember is that your balance sheet alone is not enough to determine the real value of the assets.

2. *What do these assets earn for the business?* Some assets, like specialized machinery, have little market value but produce products that earn high profit. Excess inventory, on the other hand, technically has market value but may cost a company more in interest costs and spoilage to carry than it will earn when it eventually sells. In the case of our two examples, let's assume that Company A operates at a substantial loss. This means that even though the assets on the balance sheet are valuable, they aren't doing Company A any good and might better be liquidated.

The point here is that for assets to have value to a business and to a buyer, they must earn money.

WHAT A BUSINESS EARNS

Profit and cash performance is the second key indicator of a company's value and another case in which isolated analysis is misleading. The profit on the accounting statement must first be adjusted to show the owner's real cash flow. Then the adjusted cash flow is measured as a return on the investment tied up in the business.

Buyers know that business owners, particularly those who run small businesses, often treat income and expenses in ways that minimize their total taxes. They may over- or underpay themselves. They may lavish perquisites on themselves and their families, or they may have everyone working for nothing. They may make substantial reinvestments in the business, which they treat as expenses. Further adjustments need to be made for extraordinary items, both good and bad. Strikes and fires as well as the capital gain on the sale of an asset need to be disclosed. Profits must be adjusted in order for the buyer to gain a true picture of a business's performance. The rule is simply to determine the true required cost and adjust accordingly. The result is adjusted owner's cash flow.

Our definition of *adjusted owner's cash flow* is the cash available to an owner after adjusting expenses to the level that is actually required for the business and after allowing an appropriate salary for the owner's effort in the business. This adjusted owner's cash flow is calculated with no allowance for interest or depreciation; that is, any interest or depreciation is added back as a plus to cash flow. The result is cash available to the owner or the buyer for reinvestment, growth, taxes, debt repayment, or dividends. Here are two examples of income statements that have been adjusted.

The adjusted income statement for Company X, shown in Table 3–3, is a fairly typical example of a small business in which the owner has taken a larger salary and more benefits than would be truly required if a paid manager were used. Several other expense items were higher than the business really required:

- Travel and entertainment were excessive.
- Household utilities were charged to the business, as was personal insurance.
- The automobile was completely unnecessary, but was charged to the business. Its cost was removed.
- Half of the legal and accounting expenses were nonbusiness.
- Donations were treated as expenses. By definition, these are not required expenses.
- The happy outcome here is an adjusted cash flow of $82,000 in excess of the stated profit.

TABLE 3–3   Adjusted Income Statement for Company X

	Per statement	True required cost	Adjustment
Sales	$500,000	$500,000	0
Cost of goods sold	$200,000	$200,000	0
Gross profit	$300,000	$300,000	0
Expenses:			
Employee salaries	$100,000	$100,000	0
Employee benefits	25,000	25,000	0
Owner/manager's salaries	75,000	30,000	+$45,000
Owner/manager's benefits	11,000	5,000	+$ 6,000
Travel/entertainment	15,000	5,000	+$10,000
Rent	15,000	15,000	0
Utilities and telephone	12,000	10,000	+$ 2,000
Selling expenses	5,000	5,000	0
Insurance	8,000	7,000	+$ 1,000
Automobile	9,000	0	+$ 9,000
Legal/accounting	12,000	6,000	+$ 6,000
Donations	3,000	0	+$ 3,000
Total expenses	$290,000	$208,000	+$82,000
Income before interest, depreciation, reinvestment, and taxes	$ 10,000		
Adjustments			+$82,000
Cash available		$ 92,000	

At the other extreme is Company Y, shown in Table 3–4. A major adjustment ($36,000) was required because the owner improperly chose to treat the employees as contractors and did not provide proper withholding and insurance. It often happens that the owner of a small business takes no salary even though he or she may work full time at it. Table 3–4 shows the adjustment required to provide a fair salary and benefits. In this case the owner also owns the building and charges the business less than fair market rent. Some adjustments require judgment. In this case the owner was spending nothing on sales and marketing and an adjustment was made to the budget to provide $12,000. The only minor positive adjustment was for slightly excessive travel and entertainment expenses. What initially appeared to be $103,000 in profit turns out to be only a break-even cash flow.

Our examples have shown figures for only one year of business. Buyers will expect to see several years, preferably five, to help them

TABLE 3–4	**Adjusted Income Statement for Company Y**		
	Per statement	**True required cost**	**Adjustment**
Sales	$750,000	$750,000	0
Cost of goods sold	$450,000	$450,000	0
Gross profit	$300,000	$300,000	0
Expenses:			
Employee salaries	$150,000	$150,000	0
Employee benefits	0	36,000	–$36,000
Owner/manager's salaries	0	30,000	– 30,000
Owner/manager's benefits	0	6,000	– 6,000
Travel/entertainment	8,000	7,000	+ 1,000
Rent	12,000	32,000	– 20,000
Utilities and telephone	12,000	12,000	0
Selling expenses	0	12,000	– 12,000
Insurance	7,000	7,000	0
Automobile	0	0	0
Legal/accounting	8,000	8,000	0
Donations	0	0	0
Total expenses	$197,000	$300,000	–$103,000
Income before interest, depreciation, reinvestment, and taxes	$103,000		
Adjustments			–$103,000
Cash available		0	

spot trends, identify any nonrecurring expenses or income, and determine if any single year was exceptionally good or bad.

One final note on understanding cash flow has to do with how much cash should be put back into the business. The cash flow shown in Tables 3–3 and 3–4 is labeled "before interest, depreciation, reinvestment, and taxes." A growing company needing large inventory purchases or plant expansion may require far more cash than that being generated from operations. Buyers will ask whether this cash can be borrowed from outside or whether it will require their further cash investment.

Now that we have an understanding of how much cash is being generated, we need to look next at whether that cash flow is adequate. Simply put, will buyers see this business as a good return on the investment? Merely calculating the percentage return is not enough. Buyers want to know whether it is a good return in light of the risk they are taking.

WHAT MAKES THE BUSINESS UNIQUE

The degree of risk and desirability is the third characteristic of a business that will affect its value. All the intangibles that make a business unique become pluses and minuses when it is time to establish the degree of risk. No universal scale exists, and everyone's risk preference is different. For example, a buyer with a marketing background might view a business requiring sophisticated engineering as a high risk. An engineer might say the same thing about a restaurant.

Putting personal risk preference aside, there are some measures of risk that do have general application (see Table 3–5). Worksheet 1 will help you with a risk assessment of the business.

This is a good place to stop in this chapter to review what we have discussed. We have examined the three components that affect the value of the company:

1. What the business owns—the balance sheet

2. What the business earns—profit and cash performance

3. What makes the business unique—the degree of risk and desirability

The next step is to convert the *value* produced by these three components into *price*.

PRICING THE BUSINESS

The technique to convert the *value of assets* to their price is simple addition. Converting the *value of the cash flow* is a bit more complicated. It uses a technique called *capitalization*, which will tell us how much we should pay for a stream of cash flow. Our *evaluation of risk* will also affect the price.

After we understand the basics of converting value to price we will explore the five different pricing methods (see Figure 3–1):

1. Price based on assets, used when assets are the main value in the company

2. Price based on cash flow, used when there are few assets but strong cash flow

TABLE 3–5   Risk Assessment Table

Factor	Low risk	High risk
Company history	Long, profitable history	New or unprofitable history
Industry segment	Stable or growing, highly profitable industry	Erratic growth or decline, unstable, generally unprofitable industry
Special skills required for success	No special skills are required	Highly specialized or scarce skills are required.
Location (or lease term)	The location is excellent and can continue.	The location is unsuitable and/ or requires relocation.
Labor situation	Labor is available and labor relations are good.	Labor is scarce and/or labor relations are poor.
Management situation	The remaining management team is fully qualified and competent.	Management is not competent to run the business or is not remaining.
Return *of* investment	The buyer would be able to liquidate his or her investment for about what was paid.	The investment could be easily depleted or is nonliquid.
Return *on* investment	Market, economic, and historical factors indicate returns will continue.	There are no prospects for return without changes in the company, the market, or the economy.
Outside dependency	Most of the requirements for success are within the company's control.	Success depends on factors such as interest rates, styles and fashions, or foreign sources that are outside the company's control.
Company reputation	Well recognized and highly respected	Unknown or poorly regarded
Products or services	High value, competitive, and responsive to market needs	Poor quality and/or outdated for the market
Franchises, licenses, insurance, or bonds required	No special insurance licenses, franchises, or bonds are required.	The business requires hard-to-obtain or expensive licenses, franchises, insurance, or bonds.
Competition	Competition is limited.	Competition is intense and/or increasing.
Technology	The business is not particularly vulnerable to technological changes.	A change in technology could have a major negative impact.

3. Price based on an integrated method, where both assets and cash flow are substantial

4. Price based on duplication cost, where the alternative of starting a business is developed

5. Price based on the value of future earnings, used where the probability of such earnings is high, usually in larger companies

PRICING THE ASSETS

The asset value on the balance sheet is the least controversial to establish and convert to a price. Most assets can be counted, appraised, or evaluated. As a starting point, price can equal the fair market value. You are going to sell things a buyer will own and could resell.

In adjusting the balance sheet, re-examine the reserves and allowances. Many owners of long-established businesses overlook assets that were expensed but still have market value. Tools, dies, and spare parts are examples. Also pay close attention to the notes, both payable and receivable. If these are borrowings between the owner and the company, they probably should be removed from your transaction.

Some assets are not on the balance sheet and not as easy to value. One example is a lease that is substantially under market rate. The value of a 5-year lease on 10,000 square feet at $5 per square foot per year when the market rate is $7.50 can be significant: $2.50 x 10,000 square feet x 5 years = $125,000.

However, unless you think the buyer plans to move the business and rent out this 10,000 square feet for the profit, you shouldn't value the lease. The positive benefit is already reflected in the profit/cash flow that you are going to price next.

Other such intangibles might be the company name, the customer or client list, a patent, special computer systems, or the like. Once again, buyers tend to view these as being reflected in the profit/cash flow of the business. If these intangible assets really have any value, they will have earned a premium profit return, and you can reflect that value when you put a price on the profit/cash flow. However, sometimes sellers insist that these intangibles be assigned a price. Be prepared for buyers to ask why there is a price attached to these intangibles if the business is not earning a premium because of them.

PRICING THE CASH FLOW

Putting a price on the profit/cash flow is more art than science. In theory, we are going to *capitalize the cash flow*. That means we will divide the cash flow figure by the percentage of return on investment we think we should earn and so arrive at the price. If the cash flow is $100,000 and we want a 25 percent pre-tax return, we divide $100,000 by 0.25 and find that a buyer would have to invest $400,000 to obtain that stream of cash flow. As Table 3–6 demonstrates, the *capitalization rate (cap rate)* serves the same function as the rate of return. The task is to select the proper cap rate. That selection is very dependent upon the degree of risk.

Risk Determines the Capitalization Rate

Assume that two businesses both have cash flows of $100,000. One is a low-risk business from which a buyer would be satisfied to earn a 20 percent return while the other is a higher-risk business from which a buyer would want a 30 percent return. A buyer would be willing to pay $500,000 ($100,000 divided by 0.20) for the low-risk cash flow but only $333,333 ($100,000 divided by 0.30) for the cash flow with the higher risk.

The higher the risk, the higher the cap rate and therefore the lower the investment the buyer would make. We will use the following three extreme examples in our discussion:

1. A 15-year-old newspaper delivery service has had a solid history of profit/cash flow and earns $100,000.

2. A very large restaurant featuring the owner-chef's French menu has produced $150,000 in profit/cash flow in each of its 3 years of operation.

TABLE 3–6	Cap Rate Serves Same Function as Rate of Return		
	Investment (price)		$400,000
	Rate of return		X 2.5
	Cash flow		$100,000
	$\dfrac{\text{Cash flow}}{\text{cap rate}} =$	$\dfrac{\$100,000}{.25}$	$= \$400,000$ investment (price)

3. A specialized design engineering company builds turntables for revolving restaurants and earned $200,000 in cash flow in its first year.

Before we try to develop a cap rate for these companies, we should set a benchmark that will give us a practical frame of reference. We can use a top-grade bond: It has low risk, it's very liquid, it requires little or no time to manage, and at the time of this writing, it earns 9 percent.

Any business involves risk and takes time to manage; therefore, a buyer must demand a higher return (cap rate) on that investment. It may seem to you that the returns used as examples in this chapter are high, even adjusting for risk. The reason is liquidity. As a business broker you are about to learn that converting the investment in a business into cash is not an easy or quick process.

Lack of liquidity has another impact on price and value. For example, comparing private companies with public ones, even those in the same field, and attempting to use price/earnings as a value method is a mistake. The price earnings ratio of the public company is affected by its liquidity. The stock of a public company can be traded or sold in minutes. Buyers will pay less when they can't readily convert their investment into cash.

Our frame of reference needs one other perspective, and that is the potential for increase or decrease in the value of our investment. Our top-grade bond isn't going to go up or down in value much, except to adjust for yield. Investment in a business could multiply tenfold or be completely lost.

Now let's set some cap rates for our examples. The newspaper delivery business has very low risk. It's been around for years, no special skills are needed, and no competition is likely. The only likely risk is that the newspaper will find another firm to deliver its papers. There won't be much chance of loss or growth on our investment. Try 20 percent ($100,000 ÷ 0.20 = $500,000).

The restaurant has one big risk factor, and that is the chef-owner. If he leaves when the business is sold, the new owner will have to replace him. This is a special skill. The three-year age of the business is neither a plus nor a minus. It doesn't guarantee a following, but the equipment is new enough to be sold for a good price. If you're a chef, use 30 percent; if not, 35 percent ($150,000 ÷ 0.30 = $500,000) or ($150,000 ÷ 0.35 = $429,000).

The design engineering company is a very high-risk situation. It's new, its market is very narrow and hard to influence, and the need for special skills and relationships is high. Its assets, including its round manufacturing building, have little application to anything else. A 40 percent cap rate is not unreasonable ($200,000 ÷ 0.40 = $500,000). The examples are summarized in Table 3–7.

These examples, though realistic, were contrived to make the point that degree of risk can have an impact on the cap rate sufficient to cause three businesses with widely different cash flows to be theoretically priced the same. Worksheet 1 will help you price your cash flow.

Now we have figured out how to price assets and cash flow. If a company possessed only one or the other, coming up with a total price would be easy. Sometimes this is the case. In a service company, such as one that provides security guards, there may be no assets to speak of, and the whole price will be based on the value of the

---

TABLE 3–7   **Examples of Capitalization Rates**

Newspaper Delivery Service

Risk	low
Potential for growth or decline	low
Capitalization rate	20%

$$\frac{\text{cash flow}}{\text{cap rate}} = \frac{\$100,000}{0.20} \qquad \text{Price} = \$500,000$$

Restaurant

Risk	medium
Potential for growth or decline	medium
Capitalization rate	30%

$$\frac{\text{cash flow}}{\text{cap rate}} = \frac{\$150,000}{0.30} \qquad \text{Price} = \$500,000$$

Specialized Engineering Company

Risk	high
Potential for growth or decline	high
Capitalization rate	40%

$$\frac{\text{cash flow}}{\text{cap rate}} = \frac{\$200,000}{0.40} \qquad \text{Price} = \$500,000$$

Three businesses with widely varying cash flows are theoretically priced the same when adjusted for risk by their capitalization rates.

cash flow using the capitalization rate idea. However, because many companies do have both assets and cash flow, we need a way to price them together.

INTEGRATED PRICING

One method that values assets and cash flow in an integrated way is called the *excess earnings method*. It assigns a portion of the owner's cash flow to cover the cost of carrying the assets. For example, if the assets are valued at $400,000 and it costs 10 percent to borrow money, the first $40,000 of cash flow is viewed as satisfying the return on the investment in assets. Any cash flow over that amount is considered "excess." This excess is multiplied by a factor that reflects the degree of desirability (a similar process to dividing by a cap rate) to get the value of the cash flow. This figure is then added to the value of the assets to get the total price. Here is a sample calculation:

Sample Calculation 3–1

Asset value	$400,000
Prevailing interest rate	x 10%
Cost of carrying assets	$ 40,000
Owner's cash flow	$ 50,000
Less cost of carrying assets	–40,000
Excess earnings	$ 10,000
Assumed multiplier (uses a 1–6 scale to reflect desirability)*	x 3
Value of excess earnings	$ 30,000
Value of assets	+400,000
Total value of the business	$430,000

*The use of a 1–6 scale is not arbitrary. Using factors similar to those we used in our analysis of degree of risk, a business that is average in risk and desirability would be rated 3. This multiplying by 3 gives the same result as dividing by a cap rate of 33 percent, which reflects the return most buyers would want on a business with an average degree of risk.

In cases in which the earnings are negative or not enough to carry the cost of the assets, the business is considered to be worth less than even the value of the assets, as shown in Sample Calculation 3–2.

Sample Calculation 3–2	
Asset value	$400,000
Interest rate	x 10%
Cost of carrying assets	$ 40,000
Owner's cash flow	$ 25,000
Less cost of carrying assets	–40,000
Excess earnings (negative)	$(15,000)
(Assumed multiplier cannot be used with negative excess earnings)	
Value of excess earnings	(15,000)
Value of assets	+400,000
Total value of the business	$385,000

DUPLICATION COST PRICING

Another concept to apply to the value and price of a business is *duplication cost*. The idea is to calculate what it would cost to duplicate your client's *present* business. The part of the calculation relating to assets and costs is fairly easy. Buyers can price assets that are in similar condition and can assume some level of working capital. They can determine a good price for real estate and the costs for labor, insurance utilities, and so forth. The problem comes in trying to calculate how long it would take for them to gear up any company to the level of operations and profitability of the seller's company.

Some companies may be easy to duplicate or even surpass. New businesses, poorly run or badly located businesses, and businesses requiring little know-how are examples. If a company is efficient, well established, and profitable, it could take years of operation to achieve a similar position. During these years a buyer could suffer low earnings or even losses. And while the buyer might have avoided a high front-end cash investment, he or she may end up putting as much or more cash into the business.

Duplication cost relates to the concept of the *learning curve* and its impact on efficiency. The assumption is that experience has a value and there is a cost to obtain it. Before coming to any conclusion about the price of a business you should consider what it would take to duplicate it. Your Worksheet 1 can help.

PRICING THE VALUE OF FUTURE EARNINGS

This pricing technique is called the *net present value* (NPV) method, and it involves five steps:

1. Adjust the company's statements to show true present profit.
2. Develop growth plans (plans must be supportable by evidence).
3. Project growth plans for five years.
4. Calculate profit, investments, and returns for the five years.
5. Discount the figures to the present using a discount rate that reflects the degree of risk and projected inflation. Typically this rate is 50% above the prime interest rate. Table 3–8 shows a sample calculation.

TABLE 3–8 **Net Present Value (NPV) Calculation**

Present Value of a Future $1

Discount Rate Percentage

Year	12	13	14	15	16
1	0.893	0.865	0.877	0.870	0.862
2	0.797	0.783	0.769	0.756	0.743
3	0.712	0.693	0.675	0.658	0.641
4	0.636	0.613	0.592	0.572	0.552
5	0.567	0.543	0.519	0.497	0.476

Pricing Calculation

Year	Projected earnings	X	Discounted @ 15	NPV
1	$100,000	X	0.870	$ 87,000
2	110,000	X	0.756	83,160
3	125,000	X	0.658	82,250
4	140,000	X	0.572	80,080
5	155,000	X	0.497	77,035
Total	$630,000			$409,525

NPV is used when a company's future is credible. The technique has two weaknesses:

1. The projections are always speculative.
2. Picking the discount rate is subjective.

This method is the most controversial of all methods, due to these weaknesses. Proponents argue that buyers should be willing to pay for more than just one year's earnings. They assert that paying a discounted net present value of five year's earnings is a fair price because it reflects payment for the company's momentum, its on-going value. Opponents say that owners can make plans and projections showing any growth and profitability they choose simply by making assumptions that support the growth. Opponents of NPV pricing don't believe in paying for earnings that have not yet been earned.

OTHER PRICING CONCEPTS

You should be aware of some other concepts that relate to value, price, and cash needs.

Potential and Projections

The first concept has to do with "potential." A business may have few assets and little cash flow, but through either the buyer's special skills, some unexploited attribute of the business, or some change i the business's environment, projected future growth is a high probability.

There are two ways to deal with potential. One is to use the concept of variable pricing presented later in this chapter. Ask for payment of a higher price if the growth projection does, in fact, occur. The opposite view of potential gives it no value or price to the seller. After all, it's the buyer who will do the work, take the risk, make the (possibly substantial) investment, and manage the realization of any potential.

The latter point of view is the more common, but there are plenty of cases in which some event—such as the construction of a new highway or the demise of a major competitor—just about insures growth with little cost or effort. Either way, buyers of smaller companies are normally reluctant to pay for potential before it is realized.

Occasionally the source of potential value can be identified. For example, if a company has just made an investment in a machine that is certain to produce earnings or savings, there can be *an expected value*. Another special kind of potential is *conditional value*. This refers to the value that will result if some future act occurs. An example would be a large pending contract. Conditional value can also be negative; buyers may point out that the company could lose a large customer, too.

Supply and Demand

This very basic aspect of pricing is often overlooked when pricing a business. *Supply and demand* is at work in this environment just as it is elsewhere. It has direct effects on businesses of the same and similar types. Two restaurants, if similar enough to both be considered by a buyer, will compete for sale and the price will be affected by this competition. Supply and demand has indirect effects, too. Right now, manufacturing businesses are in high demand. Business brokers attribute the demand to the surge in corporate executives' layoffs and cutbacks. Many of these executives equate "business" with "manufacturing." Premiums will be paid for manufacturing businesses as long as demand remains so strong. At the other extreme are small video rental stores, which are now in overabundant supply and often sell at a discount.

Special Factors of Value

Another concept to consider involves special factors that make the business worth a premium. A large backlog of business or an ongoing contract are two examples. Synergy, the elimination of a competitor, obtaining some special license, or even emotional factors may make the business worth a higher price to some buyers. Some sellers feel they should ask for some money for "the going business" or "the good will." What those sellers mean is there should be some price paid for all those intangibles such as the business name and reputation, the customer list, the business systems and controls, and all the other valuable elements that have been assembled over the years. Buyers are willing to pay for them and in fact *are* paying for them if they offer more than the value of the tangible assets. As mentioned earlier, if these intangible assets really do have any value, they have been earning income for the business. Whether the buyer capitalized the cash flow or used a pricing method that integrated the value of assets and the value of earnings, the buyer has given value for the intangibles. If you wish, you can call this premium over tangible asset value *goodwill* or *the key* or the *going business value*.

BUYERS PRICING TESTS

Buyers are going to perform several calculations and tests regarding the price of the business. Some are the tests used in standard financial analysis. Buyers and their advisors have access to standard industry ratios for businesses. The ratios include balance sheet ratios (current ratio, assets to sales, etc.) and income statement ratios (expense ratios to sales, margins, etc.). If you have never seen a reference book on ratios or if you want to see how your client's business compares to others in its industry, you can obtain such statistics through the Small Business Administration and the Department of Commerce. Two comprehensive sources of ratios are *The Almanac of Business and Industrial Ratios* and *Financial Studies of the Small Business*.*

In the case of smaller companies, buyers are going to test first against other alternatives. They will decide how the price, returns, and effort required in the business measure up to other investments of their time and money. The second test is described in the Institute of Business Appraisers publication MO-9 as "The Justification of Purchase Test." It states that a business should be able to provide:

- Sufficient cash to repay the loan to the seller
- Sufficient cash to support the operations of the business
- A reasonable return on the buyer's down payment
- A fair salary for the owner's work in the business

Figure 3–1 summarized these tests.

---

*Troy, Leo: *Almanac of Business and Industrial Ratios* (Englewood Cliffs, NJ: Prentice-Hall), *Financial Studies of the Small Business* (Winter Haven, FL: Financial Research Associates).

The tests on larger companies are more concerned with the futurity of the investment. With larger companies, the future outcomes are more likely to be predictable. One test involves the *cost savings value* concept mentioned earlier. When the buyer is another company, these savings may allow the buyer to justify a higher price than otherwise. Decisions regarding the price of larger companies are heavily weighted by projections of future earnings and values, using the NPV method of pricing.

Now that we have spent time on methods of arriving at a price, we will turn to the idea of affordability.

WHAT THE BUYER CAN AFFORD

Some sellers feel that the buyer's ability to pay for the business is not their concern. Any buyer who cannot afford the business is not a real buyer, as far as the seller is concerned.

The fact is, the seller and the value of the business affect its affordability to a buyer in several ways. If the business has assets of value, the buyer can borrow money against them. When you set a lower guaranteed price and allow for higher payment on some contingent basis you have made the business more affordable. The most important step the seller can take to make the business more affordable is to extend favorable terms of sale.

TERMS OF SALE

Terms of sale are:

- the portion of cash down payment
- the length of time of repaying the balance
- the interest rate
- the form of payments
  interest only
  fully ammortizing
  partially ammortizing with a balloon payment

No stronger statement about the impact of terms can be made than this: "You may set the price if I may set the terms." After all, payment terms of no cash down, no security, minimum interest, and terms that stretch for decades would make almost any price acceptable.

What the buyer can afford to pay and will be willing to pay depends much more on the actual cash required than on the price. The terms of sale can range from all cash at closing to no cash down with payment over several decades. In theory, any all-cash price can be converted to a price involving payment terms over time by using standard payment tables for any specified interest rate. All-cash terms demand the lowest selling price but will of course result in the highest cash in your seller's hand at closing. Terms affect not only affordability but buyers' perceptions of how financially attractive a deal is.

Buyers often measure the return on their investment in cash terms. Here is an example of the impact of financing on such a buyer's calculations.

1. Terms: all cash
   Cash price of business $500,000
   Cash return $100,000

$$\frac{\$100,000}{\$500,000} = 20\% \text{ return on investment}$$

2. Terms: with 2/3 financing, 10 years, 10% interest rate
   1/3 cash down payment $166,666
   Cash return $100,000
   Minus loan repayment   − $44,067

   Net cash return $55,933

$$\frac{\$55,933}{\$166,666} = 30\% \text{ return on investment}$$

Whether or not you agree with the arithmetic, you must be aware that this is often a buyer's perception, and *the buyer's perception is the buyer's reality*.

When calculating the impact of terms on the selling price, four variables are involved.

1. The cash down payment
2. The length of time for repayment
3. The interest rate

4. Whether the payments are fully amortizing or involve a large (balloon) payment at the end of the term

If you work with loan tables and do a few calculations, you will develop a general feel for the impact of certain changes in these variables. Figure 3–2 and Table 3–9 give you some idea of the impact of trade-offs. They show why hard bargaining for a point or two of

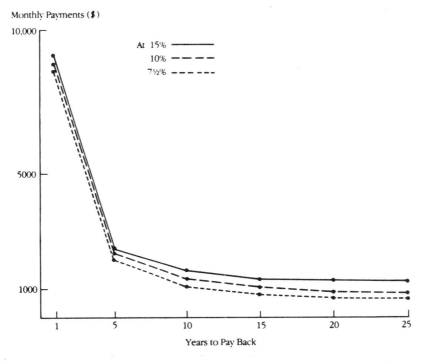

Figure 3–2. Repayment of $100,000. C.D. Peterson, *How to Leave Your Job and Buy a Business of Your Own* (New York: McGraw-Hill, 1988). Used by permission.

TABLE 3–9	Monthly Payments to Repay $100,000		
Years	**7.5%**	**10%**	**15%**
1	8676	8792	9026
5	2004	2125	2379
10	1188	1322	1613
15	928	1075	1400
20	806	965	1316
25	739	908	1280

interest may earn your seller less than what you concede to get them. Beyond the conversion of a cash price to payments by using payment tables, sellers are willing to accept a lower *real* price for an all cash transaction and want a premium if they provide extended terms. The sellers of small businesses usually do offer to finance part of the purchase, as we will see.

A major consideration about terms from your standpoint is security. Your seller wants to sell the business *and wants to get paid for it*. Structuring your transaction to provide security is vital.

USING THE VALUE OF THE BUSINESS TO IMPROVE AFFORDABILITY

The assets and liabilities from the balance sheet can be involved in helping to close the sale. Most sales of small businesses are sales of assets, not sales of stock. The buyer pays for the assets, and the seller discharges the liabilities. When the buyer agrees to discharge the liabilities, he or she only pays for the difference between the assets and liabilities, and thus is required to turn over less cash to the seller. Of course, these liabilities will have to be paid at some time, and the creditors often have to agree to the arrangement.

Another way to use the balance sheet is for the buyer to arrange, coincidental with the purchase, to borrow against the assets of the business, provided he or she hasn't pledged the assets to you. As a frame of reference, banks and others will usually lend the following percentages of value:

Machinery and equipment	50%
Inventory	50%
Accounts Receivable	50–75%

The buyer also may be able to borrow against an order backlog or special contract. Selling assets and then renting or leasing them provides another source of cash. The obvious example is real estate, but machinery, office equipment, and even telephone systems can be leased. If suppliers will provide inventory, on consignment and allow the buyer to pay the seller for the inventory as it is used and reordered, the buyer can reduce his or her cash requirement. If there is a patent that makes up a substantial part of the price, the buyer could let the seller keep the patent and instead set up a license to use it and pay a royalty. Borrowing against assets as a part of the purchase transaction can be coupled with the outright sale of some assets to generate cash. Unused real estate or an unwanted line of business are two examples.

While these ideas on balance-sheet financing are valid, they are not appropriate in every situation. The returns projected and the basic soundness of the buyer's business financing strategy should ultimately govern any actions.

VARIABLE, OR CONTINGENT PRICING

Variable pricing is a way to structure terms, not a way to set a price. Using this arrangement, the price established for the business varies in relation to some future event. The most common factor is sales volume.

Variable pricing tied to sales can be used when present sales are below historic patterns and the seller claims that some unusual event or now-solved problem was responsible. The buyer can agree to an added payout schedule if sales materialize at certain levels. Price can be tied to other variable factors, such as the number of employees who remain with the company for some time (important to real estate firms) or the number of accounts who continue with the company (important to advertising agencies).

Variable pricing can be a powerful way of adding to the real price while keeping the buyer's front-end cash requirements down. Sometimes it is the only method able to provide fairness to both parties. As you see, the terms of sale really can have a substantial impact on the affordability of your client's business.

PRICING CASE STUDY

This case study prices the Hillcrest Corporation using five different pricing methods:

1. Price based on assets
2. Price based on cash flow
3. Price based on the integrated method
4. Price based on duplication cost
5. Price based on net present value of future earnings

These two most common pricing tests will also be applied:

1. The alternative investment test
2. The reasonableness of purchase test

PART ONE—BACKGROUND

The Hillcrest Corporation is a 10-year-old manufacturer of fishing rods and other tackle for saltwater fishing. The operations of the company are sound, and growth in sales and profit has been steady. The industry has been experiencing growth for many years, and future prospects look good.

The owner has trained his 15 employees well. Although he is still the key manager of the company, he has provided for a good manager as his replacement. The owner has taken only a token salary, but he and his family have taken perks and made some discretionary charges to the business. Most of these can be identified.

The company's machinery and equipment are standard metal and woodworking devices. Both are nearly fully depreciated, but they have a ready market value. Competitors, particularly the Japanese, are beginning to use high-tech equipment and exotic materials.

Distribution is made through wholesalers. Competition is strong but not predatory. The business operates one shift five or six days per week, depending on demand, which is somewhat seasonal.

The real estate, a modern 20,000 sq. ft. factory with a sales office, is owned by the business owner personally. He has not been charging the business any rent. The real estate is not to be included in the sale of the business. Two luxury cars are leased by the company for the use of the owner and his wife.

PART TWO—FINANCIAL STATEMENTS AND ADJUSTMENTS

A. Hillcrest Corporation Balance Sheet as of Dec. 31, 19__

	Per Statement	Adjusted
ASSETS		
Current Assets:		
Cash	$ 50,000	$ 50,000
Accounts receivable	250,000	250,000
Notes receivable	20,000	0[1]
Inventories	75,000	80,000[2]
Prepaid expenses	10,000	10,000
Other	—	—
Total Current Assets	$ 405,000	$ 390,000
Fixed Assets:		
Furniture, machinery, & equipment	$1,960,000	
Less accumulated depreciation	(1,560,000)	
Total Fixed Assets	$ 400,000	$1,110,000[3]
Total Assets	$805,000	$1,500,000

[1] Note receivable is a loan to the present owner and can just be removed.
[2] Inventory was kept LIFO, and the older material has a higher than book value.
[3] This is the real market value of the highly salable standard equipment and machinery.

LIABILITIES		
Current Liabilities:		
Accounts payable	$ 80,000	$ 80,000
Wages payable	32,000	32,000
Taxes payable	49,000	49,000
Interest payable	1,000	1,000
Notes/leases (current portion)	38,000	38,000
Services or products owed to customers	—	—
Other liabilities	—	—
Total Current Liabilities	$200,000	$200,000
Long Term Liabilities:		
Notes/leases	$190,000	$190,000
Mortgages	—	—
Other	—	—
Total Liabilities	$390,000	$390,000
Owner's Equity:		
Capital Stock	$1,000	$1,000
Retained earnings	414,000	1,109,000
Total Owner's Equity	$415,000	$1,110,000

B. Hillcrest Corporation Income (P & L) Statement for the period Jan. 1, 19__ to Dec. 31, 19__

	Per Statement	Adjusted
Sales:	$2,000,000	$2,000,000
Less cost of sales (45%)	900,000	900,000
Gross profit (55%)	$1,110,000	$1,110,000
Expenses:		
Owner's salary	$ 10,000	$ 45,000[4]
Owner's benefits	2,000	12,000[4]
Employee salaries (15)	345,000	345,000
Employee benefits	84,000	84,000
Rent	0	120,000[5]
Utilities	20,000	20,000
Travel & entertainment	23,000	10,000[6]
Selling expenses	32,000	32,000
Depreciations	10,000	10,000
Insurance	12,000	7,000[7]
Interest	10,000	10,000
Auto expense	16,000	0[8]
Legal and accounting	10,000	5,000[9]
Other	12,000	0[10]
Total Expenses	$ 586,000	$ 700,000
Pretax Profit:	$ 514,000	$ 400,000

[4] The salary and benefits are adjusted to show a fair salary to a full time owner-manager.
[5] The rent is adjusted up to show a reasonable rate of $6.00 per foot x 20,000 sq. ft.
[6] Excessive travel and entertainment is adjusted down to a reasonable level.
[7] Home and other personal insurance has been charged to the business, amount is adjusted down.
[8] No cars are necessary in Hillcrest Corporation, they are eliminated.
[9] Personal legal and accounting services are charged to the business and are adjusted out.
[10] "Other represents donations to the owner's favorite causes. They are not required and are eliminated."

C. Hillcrest Corporation Adjusted Owner's Cash flow For the period Jan. 1, 19__ to Dec. 31, 19__

Adjusted Profit	$400,000
Interest paid on loans	10,000
Depreciation	10,000
Further adjustments to salaries	0
Other adjustments	0
Adjusted Owner's Cash Flow	$ 420,000

D. Hillcrest Corporation Risk Assessment Worksheet

Risk Factor	Rated 1 to 6 (6 is low risk)
Company history	5
The industry segment	3
Special skills required	3
Location/lease terms	3
Special relationships required	3
Labor situation	4
Management situation	4
Return *of* investment	2
Return *on* investment	3
Outside dependency	3
Company reputation	3
Products or services	2
Licenses, insurance required	3
Competition	2
Technology	2
Total	45

Divided by 15 = the average which is the desirability multiplier = 3

PART 3—PRICING CALCULATIONS

1. Price based on assets

Estimated market value of assets from adjusted balance sheet	$1,500,000
Less liabilities being assumed	0
Price based on assets	$1,500,000

2. Price based on cash flow

Owner's cash flow from adjusted financial statements	$420,000
Capitalization rate (cap rate) based on desired return on investment. (This is a business of average risk, and we have chosen an average rate of return.)	30%

   Price based on cash flow:

   $$\frac{\$420,000}{.30} = \$1,400,000$$

3. Price based on the integrated method

Market value of assets	$1,500,000
Prevailing borrowing rate – 12%	X .12
Cost of carrying assets	$180,000
Adjusted owner's cash flow	$420,000
Less: Cost of carrying assets	– 180,000
Excess earnings	$240,000
Desirability multiplier from risk assessment worksheet	X 3
Value of excess earnings	$ 720,000
Plus: Market value of assets	+ 1,500,000
Price based on integrated method	$2,220,000

4. Price based on duplication costs

It is assumed it will take five years to reach the present level of cash flow of Hillcrest Corporation.

The assets will be purchased at market value $1,500,000

The losses during the five years will accumulate as follows:

Year	Cash Flow from the business	Lost salary from employment	
1	– $600,000	– 50,000 =	$650,000
2	– 400,000	– 50,000 =	450,000
3	+ 100,000	– 50,000 =	+ 50,000
4	+ 200,000	–	= +200,000
5	+ 400,000	–	= +400,000
	Total losses		$ 450,000
	Approximate[1] duplication cost		$1,950,000

[1] The duplication cost can only be approximate because of the uncertainty of the projected time and losses to grow the new business. Mathematical adjustments for present value are ignored.

5. Price based on net present value (NPV) of future earnings.

Hillcrest Corporation has prepared a five year plan that, based on available industry statistics, calls for the company to:

• Enter the market for freshwater fishing equipment
• Add fishing reels to the product line
• Develop a catalog selling division

Investment would be modest, and the factory still has capacity on the second and third shifts. Growth in adjusted profits is projected at a rate of 20% per year.

Present	Year 1	Year 2	Year 3	Year 4	Year 5	Total
$400,000	$480,000	$576,000	$691,000	$829,000	$995,000	3,571,000

Discount rate is 15% (50% above prime rate), so discount factor from Table 3–2 is

	X .870	X .756	X .658	X .572	X .497
NPV is	$418,000	$435,000	$455,000	$474,000	$495,000

Price based on net present value is $2,277,000

6. The alternative investment test

We determine that the buyer could invest his or her money at 10% and could earn about $50,000 in a job.

Hillcrest Corporation provides an adjusted owner's cash flow of $420,000 which includes a salary of $45,000.

This is what the buyer could earn in his or her other investments at the various prices we have developed.

Price based on assets	$1,500,000	
Invested at 10% =	150,000	
Plus salary from job =	50,000	
Total from the alternative		$200,000

Price based on cash flow	$1,400,000	
Invested at 10% =	140,000	
Plus salary from job =	50,000	
Total from the alternative		$190,000

Price based on integrated method	$2,220,000	
Invested at 10% =	220,000	
Plus salary from job =	50,000	
Total from the alternative		$270,000

Price based on NPV	$2,277,000	
Invested at 10% =	227,700	
Salary from job =	50,000	
Total		$277,700

The tests show that at every price we have developed, Hillcrest Corporation is a better investment than the alternatives. Of course, it should be better to compensate for the risk, effort, and lack of liquidity that the alternatives do not have.

At the highest price we have developed, Hillcrest Corporation provides a return of 18.4%

$$\frac{\$420,000 \text{ cash flow}}{\$2,277,000 \text{ highest price}} = 18.4\% \text{ return}$$

7. The reasonableness of purchase test

We will assume that the highest price
we developed is being paid all in cash. $2,277,000

Can the adjusted cash flow of $ 420,000
1. Support itself?
   (Depreciation is covered)   —
2. Provide a Salary?
   (A fair salary is provided in the expenses)   —
3. Pay the purchase debt?
   (There is no purchase debt)   —
4. Cover the equivalent of the lost interest
   on the cash payment?

   $2,227,000 x 10% $ 227,700

Even at its highest price, Hillcrest Corporation passes the test for reasonableness.

WORKSHEET 1

Pricing the Business

A. What the Business Owns (pricing the assets):

Detail of individual asset or liability value adjustments:

Asset or Liability Name	Reason for Adjustment	Value per Statement	Amount of Adjustment (+ or −)	Estimated Market Value
_____	_____	$_____	$_____	$_____
_____	_____	_____	_____	_____
_____	_____	_____	_____	_____
_____	_____	_____	_____	_____
_____	_____	_____	_____	_____
_____	_____	_____	_____	_____
_____	_____	_____	_____	_____
_____	_____	_____	_____	_____
_____	_____	_____	_____	_____
_____	_____	_____	_____	_____
_____	_____	_____	_____	_____
_____	_____	_____	_____	_____
_____	_____	_____	_____	_____

Balance Sheet

as of _____

ASSETS	Per Statement	Adjustments	Estimated Market Value
Current Assets:			
Cash	$ _____	$ _____	$ _____
Accounts receivable	_____	_____	_____
Notes receivable	_____	_____	_____
Inventory	_____	_____	_____
Prepaid expenses	_____	_____	_____
Other	_____	_____	_____
Total Current Assets	$ _____	$ _____	$ _____
Fixed Assets:			
Furniture, fixtures, machinery & equipment, net of depreciation	$ _____	$ _____	$ _____
Land and buildings, net of depreciation	_____	_____	_____
Other assets	_____	_____	_____
Total Fixed Assets	$ _____	$ _____	$ _____
Total Assets	$ _____	$ _____	$ _____
Current Liabilities:			
Accounts payable	$ _____	$ _____	$ _____
Wages payable	_____	_____	_____
Taxes payable	_____	_____	_____
Interest payable	_____	_____	_____
Notes/leases (current portion)	_____	_____	_____
Services or products owed to customers	_____	_____	_____
Other liabilities	_____	_____	_____
Total Current Liabilities	$ _____	$ _____	$ _____
Long-term Liabilities:			
Notes	$ _____	$ _____	$ _____
Mortgages	_____	_____	_____
Other _____	_____	_____	_____
Total Long-term Liabilities	$ _____	$ _____	$ _____
Owner's Equity:			
Capital stock	$ _____	$ _____	$ _____
Retained earnings	_____	_____	_____
Total Owner's Equity	$ _____	$ _____	$ _____
Total Liabilities & Owner's Equity	$ _____	$ _____	$ _____

Summary of Value

Assets being purchased (market value)	$ _____
Less: liabilities being assumed (market value)	_____
Reasonable Price Based on Assets	$ _____

B. What the Business Earns (pricing the cash flow):

The Income (P&L) Statement

for the Period _____ to _____

	Per Statement	Adjustment	Adjusted Figure
Sales	$ _____		
Cost of sales	$ _____		
Gross Profit	$ _____		
Expenses:			
Owner's salary	$ _____	$ _____	$ _____
Owner's benefits	_____	_____	_____
Employee salaries			
(no. of people _____)	_____	_____	_____
Employee benefits	_____	_____	_____
Rent	_____	_____	_____
Utilities	_____	_____	_____
Travel & entertainment	_____	_____	_____
Selling expenses	_____	_____	_____
Depreciation	_____	_____	_____
Insurance	_____	_____	_____
Interest	_____	_____	_____
Automobile	_____	_____	_____
Legal and accounting	_____	_____	_____
Other _____	_____	_____	_____
Other _____	_____	_____	_____
Other _____	_____	_____	_____
Total Expenses	$ _____	$ _____	$ _____
Pretax Profit	$ _____	$ _____	$ _____

Owner's Cash Flow Calculation

Adjusted profit shown on above financial statement	$ _____
Interest paid on loans	_____
Depreciation	_____
Salaries/wages paid to persons not required in business	_____
Change in rent because of new owner (+ or –)	_____
Expense of previous nonrecurring items (e.g., computers,)	_____
Other adjustments (+ or –)	
_____	_____
_____	_____
_____	_____
_____	_____
_____	_____
_____	_____
Adjusted Owner's Cash Flow	$ _____

C. What Makes the Business Unique (risk assessment):

Risk Factor	Your Candidate Rank (1 to 6; 6 is low risk)
Company history	_____
The industry segment	_____
Special skills required	_____
Location/lease terms	_____
Special relationships required	_____
Labor situation	_____
Management situation	_____
Return *of* investment	_____
Return *on* investment	_____
Outside dependency	_____
Company reputation	_____
Products or services	_____
Franchises, licenses, insurance, or bonds required	_____
Competition	_____
Technology	_____
Total	_____

Divide total by 15 for overall risk assessment
(This is also known as the *desirability multiplier*).

_____

D. Pricing Calculations

1. Assets
   Market value of assets $ _____
   Less: liabilities being assumed   − _____
       Price based on assets $ [_____]

2. Cash flow
   Adjusted owner's cash flow $ _____
   Divided by: capitalization rate   _____
       (the rate of return you want on this business)
       Price based on capitalization of cash flow $ [_____]

3. Duplication
   Cost to buy assets at market value $ _____
   Plus: start-up costs as follows:

Year	Business Losses		Lost Earnings		Annual Costs
1	$ _____	+	$ _____	=	$ _____
2	_____	+	_____	=	_____
3	_____	+	_____	=	_____
4	_____	+	_____	=	_____
5	_____	+	_____	=	_____
N	_____	+	_____	=	_____
Total	$ _____	+	$ _____	=	→ $ _____

Price based on duplication $ [_____]

4. Integrated method

Market value of assets	$ _____
Times: prevailing commercial interest rate	x _____ %
Cost of carrying assets	$ _____
Owner's cash flow	$ _____
Less: cost of carrying assets	− _____
Excess earnings	$ _____
Times: desirability multiplier (from item C)	x _____
Value of excess earnings	$ _____
Plus: market value assets	+ _____
Price based on integrated method	$

The candidate company has special value because of some unique advantage it can provide (i.e., cost savings, elimination of competition, a hard-to-obtain franchise or license, a valuable location, etc.).

Price premium for special value $

5. Discounted cash flow method

Projected cash flow	Year 1	2	3	4	5	Total
	$___	$___	$___	$___	$___	
Time discount	X.___	X___	X___	X.___	X.___	
Discounted cash flow	___	___	___	___	___	$___

Price based on five years discounted cash flow $

E. Pricing Tests

1. Alternative investment test:

The present rate of return on a bank CD	_____ %
Salary you could earn as an employee	$ _____
Compared to:	
Rate of return on candidate company:	
Owner's cash flow divided by proposed selling price	_____ %
Owner's salary and cash flow	$ _____

2. Justification of Purchase Test

Owner's cash flow from B above $ _____
(includes a salary of $_____)
Plus:
    Cash to be gained by selling unneeded assets $ _____
    Cash to be gained by trimming inventories   _____
    Cash to be gained by extending payables   _____
    Other cash to be gained   _____
Total cash to be gained $ _____

Less:
    Cash needed to repay debt $ _____
    Cash needed for additional salary   _____
    Cash needed for repairs or replacement   _____
    Cash needed to increase inventories   _____
    Cash needed to increase accounts receivable   _____
    Cash needed to compensate for the interest that
        could have been earned on the down payment   _____
Total cash needed $ _____

Actual cash available (or required) $ _____

3. First year cash evaluation of purchase
    Actual cash available (as above) (A) $ _____
Divided by:
    Cash down payment $ _____
    Plus:
        Additional cash invested or loaned $ _____
    Total cash put into the business (B) $ _____

Cash on cash return (year 1 only) (A) ÷ (B)   _____ %

From *How to Sell Your Business* by C. D. Peterson, published by the McGraw-Hill Book Company. Copyright © 1990 McGraw-Hill, Inc. Reprinted with permission.

4

Listings

Listings, what you have available for sale, are just as important in selling business opportunities as they are in selling real estate. Good listings attract buyers *and* other listings. Finding potential business sellers involves some variations on the accepted farming techniques used in real estate. Converting these potential sellers, once they are found, into listings requires only some small modifications to the well-known listing presentation.

First, you will need to get set up in business, develop contacts, and conduct an active search. Figure 4–1 outlines how to develop a pool of candidates. You are going to follow all of these procedures in your farming, but rather than doing it only once, you will be repeating your search on a regular planned basis. In the process you will be making contact with a great number of potential sellers, intermediaries, advisors, and others. It is important that you establish your credibility with them and be recognized as a business person of substance.

GETTING ESTABLISHED

Listing and selling businesses is not as common an activity as selling real estate. Many people will need to be told exactly what your function is and how it can benefit them. You can establish credibility

Preparation

Set up to manage the search
Print copies of your objectives and background
Establish clerical and phone resources
Develop a list of contact sources
    Consider newspapers, newsletters, trade magazines,
    business brokers, business owners, lawyers, accountants,
    bankers, friends, venture capitalists, networks, vendors and
    suppliers, customers, trade associations, and others.

The Active Search

Targeted Direct Marketing
    Set objectives and design overall farming program
    Direct mail
    Telephone solicitation
    Personal contact
    Define your targets for each source
    Develop lists, select desired format
    Develop messages for mail, phone, and personal contact
    Execute direct marketing search
    Mail letters, make phone calls, and knock on doors. Follow
      up
    Evaluate and develop your pool of candidates
Advertising (print is suggested)
    Decide which of your contact sources can be reached
      through advertising
    Determine how best to reach them
    Develop message(s)
    Place advertising
    Follow up
    Evaluate and develop your pool of candidates

Figure 4–1. Diagram of a Business Search

in a direct way by preparing a printed statement of your objectives
and purpose and a summary of your qualifications. This statement
can be a single-page presentation or an elaborate brochure, depending on your market and your resources. An example of a brochure
is shown as Appendix D at the back of this book. This statement of
who you are and what you can do for the seller and buyer will be
used later as part of your listing presentation.

    Indirect ways to establish credibility involve the use of quality
stationery, business cards, and businesslike telephone and office
procedures. Conducting your efforts in a businesslike manner also

means that any contact, correspondence, or follow-through is done with courtesy and professionalism.

Execute your farming crisply and with control. The easiest way to stay in control is to organize your activities into manageable segments. Direct-mail programs should be large enough to be economical, but small enough to permit telephone follow-up. A mailing of 250 with a 5 percent response rate would produce 12 to 13 responses. Personal contacts should be staggered far enough apart to permit rescheduling and to allow ample time to pursue any opportunity that might develop.

If you have a computer or your own office services, set up your planned cycles of contact, follow-up, and follow-through. If you don't have your own facilities, you can buy the services you need. In almost every city and town you can now find service companies that will type and mail to your mailing list. Most of them can maintain your mailing list and handle responses according to your instructions.

Your program should include a mix of mail, telephone, and personal contact. Farming will take time. You should view it as a long-term process of building and maintaining a network of relationships.

DEVELOPING CONTACTS AND SOURCES

PRINT MEDIA

The easiest place to start farming for businesses is in the classified section of the newspaper. You will find many businesses advertised for sale by the owner. Most of the advertisements will be for small businesses, but occasionally large opportunities will be offered. (Examples: The *Wall Street Journal*, in its "Mart" section on Wednesdays and Thursdays, lists opportunities of all sizes. The Sunday Business Opportunities sections in the *New York Times* and the *Los Angeles Times* run several pages each and contain a very diverse range of opportunities.) Specialized business opportunity newspapers are another good source. Some are national, such as The *Business Opportunity Journal*, and some, such as *The New England Business Opportunity Review*, are regional (see the Resources Literature section at the back of this book for a list of business opportunity publications).

Some banks publish newsletters of business opportunities. First

National Bank of Maryland and the Union Trust Company in Connecticut are two examples. Find out if the banks in your area provide this service.

These magazines sometimes contain a classified section with business opportunities. *Restaurant Exchange News*, a regional trade magazine, has extensive offerings. If you have narrowed your farming to a particular industry, get copies of industry trade papers and magazines. Business opportunity advertisements are usually very cryptic—only general descriptions are given. Names and location are almost never provided in order to protect the business. Severe harm could be done if customers, employees, suppliers, or competitors learned that the business was for sale.

When you answer "for sale by owner" advertisements, whether by mail or telephone, you are trying to do one thing: get an appointment. When responding by mail, be sure you present yourself as fully qualified so that the advertiser will want to contact you. If you do receive a return contact, or if you are answering the ad by telephone, you are beginning your active contact.

BUSINESS CONTACTS

Although it is not exactly farming, contacting business brokers offers the next easiest method to explore available business opportunities. Business brokers function much the same as real estate brokers, and many, though not all, will participate in cobrokerage. A business broker may have many businesses listed, but few brokers have any cooperative or multiple-listing arrangements. This means you will need to contact nearly all the business brokers in an area to learn of all the businesses listed with them. This lack of multiple listing underlines the importance of obtaining your own good listings.

Building good relationships with other business brokers should be one of your first steps. Business brokers have an extensive inventory of businesses listed for sale. They have experience that can serve you well. If brokers are willing to share their listings and their experience with you, you have a valuable resource at no cost. In return, you owe the brokers the courtesy of dealing with them honestly and the realization that, as with you, their time is money.

You should evaluate business brokers as you would any real estate firm. Get information on the competence and reputation of anyone with whom you will be working.

Even if their business isn't for sale at the time you contact them, owners can often tell you who might be selling. They can pass your name along to other owners. If they ever do decide to sell, your past contact may get you an early look at the business. Lawyers, accountants, and other personal advisors are properly protective of their clients and may be difficult to contact, but they will respond to a professional inquiry if they have a client who may be selling. Take the time to meet bankers and find out who handles business accounts. Make their acquaintance. Present your objectives and your background. You may someday be asking the bank to help you finance a deal, so your contact work can be doubly valuable.

Venture capitalists, merger and acquisition specialists, and corporate development executives can be vital sources. Whether these people exist independently or inside other companies, they all live in worlds where you may find business opportunities. Most will be interested in only large transactions. A worthwhile long shot is a call to the corporate development executive or merger and acquisition specialist inside a large company to see if the company may have a small product line or division it wants to sell.

If you know you want to focus on restaurants, for example, find the vendors and suppliers of restaurant paper supplies, meat and provisions, equipment, and so on. They have several motives for agreeing to help you. Most salespeople pride themselves on knowing what's going on in the market, and that pride is satisfied by displaying the knowledge to you. Salespeople search for ways to help their customers, and bringing a client news of someone looking to buy into their industry might be very useful. Finally, if you are successful in listing and selling a business in the industry, a salesperson who has helped you will hope that your appreciation will be reflected in recommendations to the new owner.

If you know the exact type of business you want to farm, vendors and suppliers can be a source of contacts that will put you way ahead of others who are looking for similar companies. Not only will you know about companies sooner, but your initiative and determination will be recognized as signs of your seriousness and professionalism.

Organizations and Associations

Networks that exist not as part of a club or civic group but solely as sources of business leads are a relatively new phenomenon. They were mentioned in Chapter Two as a basic part of today's business conduct. Some network groups may require that you represent a company, but many are much more informal and hold meetings that are more like mixers. Locating these groups takes some work. Start with your Chamber of Commerce and then check places where these types of meetings might be held, such as hotels and restaurants. (If no such networks exist in your area, you may want to start one.)

Industry trade associations are repositories of membership lists, statistics, and other information about the industry and the people in it. You can learn a great deal about your target industry by contacting or joining the industry's trade association. Your efforts would have both present and future benefits.

This list of sources is by no means exhaustive. Real estate and stock brokers, civic groups, the Chamber of Commerce, various state development agencies, customers, and friends are just a few additional sources you might use. The list does prove, however, that there are a great many sources for the determined business seeker. Worksheet 2 at the end of this chapter can help you organize your contacts.

Of course, just compiling an ingenious list of contact sources won't produce a pool of candidates. You have to work these contacts actively with a full program.

PROVIDING INCENTIVES FOR LEADS

Because you are asking people to do something for your economic benefit, you should be willing to compensate them.* Compensation is regulated in some states, but in others you can offer a finder's fee to those who bring you opportunities. You can pay the fee only if you actually list and sell the business, or you can encourage leads and be willing to pay if the lead simply meets your criteria. The payment for just providing leads would be relatively small, but the payment for a lead that results in the sale of a business could be several thousand dollars, depending on the size of the business.

Meaningful incentives will encourage people to make efforts they would not otherwise make and to remember you when they would otherwise forget. Paying people for their time and effort, when legally permitted, is not only fair, it is good business. You may want to make your offer of payment quietly, or you may want to make it in dramatic style by, say, offering a "$5,000 reward" in a newspaper advertisement. Be very sure you check your state laws regulating such payment before you advertise.

---

*Some people engaged in business brokerage are very much opposed to paying for leads. They view such payments as unprofessional behavior. Check the custom in your market but make your own judgments.

THE ACTIVE SEARCH

Once you have provided for your clerical and administrative needs and have generated an extensive stock of contacts, you can devise your active search and farming program (see Figure 4–1).

It's the active search and farming program that will lead you to businesses before others find them. You will even be able to find businesses that owners haven't actively tried to sell, but that are available if an offer is made. Also, your active inquiry may be the event that initiates an owner's interest in selling. To be effective, your program should use targeted direct marketing techniques and well-planned advertising.

TARGETED DIRECT MARKETING

Targeted direct marketing, as the name implies, involves your direct solicitation to specific contacts. *Direct mail* is the easiest and broadest reaching of the direct marketing techniques. *Telephone solicitation* is an effective method for a smaller and more qualified list of contacts. *Personal contact* or *canvassing* is the most powerful but most time-consuming direct-marketing activity. These three techniques are most often combined to achieve maximum effectiveness.

The six steps involved in targeted direct marketing are:

1. Setting objectives
2. Defining your targets
3. Developing your list
4. Creating your message
5. Executing the search
6. Following up and evaluating results

Setting Objectives

The kind of objectives you establish for your direct-marketing contacts will depend on the type of contact. With accountants, attorneys, vendors, trade associations, friends, and other business people who are indirectly involved, your primary objective is to learn the name of any company that may be for sale. If you can get an introduction, that's a big plus. A second objective when in contact with these people is to find others who may be helpful. The question, "Do you know anyone who . . . ," is a good network builder. A third objective is to leave a clear, positive impression with the contact so that he or she will remember to call you when a company meeting your general criteria does become available.

The objective for direct contact with brokers and other intermediaries is different. With them you must try to build a more substantive relationship. As was mentioned earlier, they can be a major resource for you. You will want to convince these intermediaries that you are a serious, qualified person who will act quickly and professionally when presented with opportunities that meet your criteria.

There are special objectives for your farming contacts with owners of businesses who might be candidates for your pool of opportunities. The overriding objective is to gain an appointment to determine whether the company is, or could be, for sale. View your efforts with these business owners as a series of contacts. Owners are cautious when discussing their businesses. You will need to earn their confidence. Earlier, we presented ways to help establish credibility (written objectives, a personal summary, business cards, etc.). Use these tools in a well-organized, professional way in your contacts with business owners.

An objective for any contact you make should be to learn as much as you can about the market and the companies in it.

Defining Your Targets

The key to success in direct marketing is the quality of your list, and the key to the quality of your list is how well you define your targets. Defining some of your targets is easy. All accountants in your geographic area are target contacts. The same may be true for attorneys, bankers, and brokers, but some contacts may need to be defined more narrowly. Using our previous example of vendors as contacts for the restaurant business, you would need to identify the vendor type (i.e., paper supplier) and the industry being served (restaurants). Consultants, venture capitalists, customers, and trade associations all need this kind of refinement to be worthwhile contacts.

Determining which companies you want to contact is not so simple. This most important category of target contacts needs the most careful definition. Fortunately you have already decided on the focus of your activities (Chapter 2), so you can now define your target companies either by size, type of business, geography, or some combination of these. The better the job you do to refine your list, the better the results of your search.

Developing Your List

The next step in your active farming search is to convert these now defined contact targets into real names, addresses, and telephone numbers. You need to develop your list, or *farm*. Working with lists has become an easier task now that personal computers are commonplace. There are several types of software on the market that permit easy construction of a mailing list. Software that allows you to generate letters, envelopes, and labels is also widely available. In addition, there are service companies that can perform all of these tasks, usually on a price-per-name basis.

The easiest way to develop a list is to buy one. List companies and brokers can supply you with lists of all the target contacts used here as examples, often customized to your specifications. The cost and quality of lists varies greatly. Prices range from $20 per thousand names to several hundred dollars per thousand. Some lists are well maintained and accurate; others are not. The list provider should advise you of the "percent deliverable" for any list you buy. A good source of help in locating and dealing with list companies is an advertising agency that is active in the direct-mail field (see the Resources Literature section at the back of this book for the names of several list companies).

You may prefer to compile your own list. Getting the names, addresses, and telephone numbers of most of your contacts should be simple. Your network of business contacts and friends is probably already formatted into a list. Compiling the list of target companies will take some effort, but not as much as you might think. There are directories of companies* for almost every industry segment imaginable. These directories can often help you zero in on such specific criteria as size, location, number of employees, and years in business. Some may even provide the names of the owners or chief executives.

Directories can be expensive to buy. Here are some suggestions of sources that may permit you to use their directories:

---

*There are actually directories of directors—see the Resources Literature section at the back of this book.

- College libraries

- Chambers of commerce

- Trade associations

- Advertising agencies

- Marketing departments of companies that sell to your target companies

In addition, there are full directory services that operate across all industries. Two of the most well known are Thomas Publishing Company, publishers of *Thomas Register*, and Dun and Bradstreet. Dun's Marketing Services, a Dun and Bradstreet division, provides standard or customized directory listings and will fill orders for mailing labels. Developing your list, then, can be as commonplace as looking in the Yellow Pages or as obscure as getting the attendance list from a conference your targets would have attended.

The last thing you need to know if you decide to order lists is that you must specify the format you want. Lists are available as magnetic (computer) tape, pressure-sensitive (peel-and-stick) labels, and Cheshire (machine-applied) labels. You might want magnetic tape if you were working with a service firm. Cheshire labels are usually cheaper but require a printer or mailer to apply them, sometimes at an extra cost. They are not economical for short runs. Pressure-sensitive labels cost more but are easy to apply. If you are doing the mailing yourself, this is the format to order.

Creating Your Message

Once you have a well-defined and usable list of contacts, you can turn to the second most important element in your direct-marketing program: your message.

The purpose of your message, just as in real estate, is to get a response. Whether you are using the mail, the telephone, or personal canvassing, you will need to put enough into your message to trigger the desired responses from the desired targets.

Some sample letters for the *direct-mail* segment of your marketing program are shown in Figures 4–2, 4–3, 4–4, and 4–5.

There are also more general farming tools, just as in real estate. A recent innovation is a quarterly business newsletter that you can purchase in bulk to use as your basic communications piece to business owners. For more information, contact the publisher:

Small Business Scene
Box 247
Concord, MA 01742

Your general farming should be made up of useful communications for the receivers and should convey your qualifications and successes.

Making "cold" telephone calls is a stomach-churning experience for many people. The prospect of personal rejection in *telephone solicitation* is both unappealing and probable. There are two things that can help you overcome the apprehension you may have. One is simply experience. People who are frightened to call strangers

---

Ms. Stephanie Stevens, Esq.
Stevens and Jones Attorneys
37 Arch Street
St. Petersburg, FL 33705

Dear Attorney Stevens:

My firm and I help people buy and sell businesses. We specialize in the St. Petersburg area. We represent many financially qualified buyers and will move quickly and professionally to examine any candidate you may bring forward. We can also provide you and your clients with pricing evaluations of businesses.

The enclosed brochure presents an outline of our services.

Please be assured that I will comply with any requirements for confidentiality you may suggest.

If you have a candidate company or would like to know more about me and my company, please write or call.

OR

I will take the liberty of calling you to explain my services more fully and to learn whether you have any clients who might be candidates.

Thank you for your consideration.

Yours truly,

Christopher Cronin

Figure 4–2. Sample Letter for Advisors

Mr. James Davis
Membership Director
Florida Building Products Association
211 Main Street
Tampa, FL 33615

Dear Mr. Davis:

My firm and I represent several financially qualified people
who are interested in buying lumberyards or buildings supply
centers in the Tampa/St. Petersburg area. Garden centers,
landscaping companies, and specialty contractors would also
be of interest.

The enclosed brochure explains more fully the services that
we offer.

Because you are a key part of the industry, I would especially
appreciate any help and advice you could give me. Please be
assured that I will comply with any requirements for confidentiality or anonymity you may suggest.

I will take the liberty of calling you to more fully explain my
objectives and to ask your advice on how to proceed.

Thank you in advance for your consideration.

Yours truly,

Christopher Cronin

Figure 4–3. Sample Letter for Vendors, Customers, Trade Associations
and so on

learn through experience that success can be achieved and failure
is anonymous.

The second key to cold calls is the use of a prepared opening
script. Experts in the field of telemarketing advise lots of rehearsal,
which will instill confidence and make you more comfortable and
natural with your presentation.

The scripts for contacting accountants, attorneys, brokers, trade
associations, vendors, and other nonowners can be paraphrases of
the direct-mail letters. The scripts for telephone contact with owners
require one major revision. Unless the owner answers the phone, you
may have trouble getting through to talk with him or her.

The following script is an example of how to approach a business
when you do not have the advantage of the owner's name:

Mr. Fred Steck
Steck's Lumber
12277 Bayside
St. Petersburg, FL 33705

Dear Mr. Steck:

My firm and I help people buy and sell businesses.

Although I have not heard that your business is for sale, I decided to approach you directly in the event you may have a desire to sell.

We represent several buyers with serious interests in lumber and building products companies. Their financial situation is solid, and they have cash available.

If your business is not for sale, perhaps you could forward this letter to another business owner who may be interested in selling. Garden centers, landscaping companies, and specialty contractors would also be of interest. A brochure describing our services, including price evaluations, is enclosed.

If you would like to know more about me and my company, please write or call.

OR

I will take the liberty of calling you to explain more fully my services and to learn whether you or someone you know may have an interest in selling.

Thank you for your consideration.

Yours truly,

Christopher Cronin

Figure 4–4. Sample Letter for Company Owners—Version 1

"Hello, my name is Chris Cronin. With whom am I speaking, please?"

"This is Bob."

"I'm trying to locate the owner of Steck's Lumberyard. Are you the owner?"

(If yes, use the "Letter to Owners" as a script. If no, continue.)

"Oh. May I ask who the owner is?"

Mr. Fred Steck
Steck's Lumber
11277 Bayside
St. Petersburg, FL 33705

Dear Mr. Steck:

Have you ever wondered what someone would pay for your business?

My firm and I specialize in helping people buy, sell, and evaluate businesses. The enclosed brochure describes what we do.

As a part of our services, we would be pleased to conduct a (free) confidential market evaluation of your business. If you would like to know how buyers would evaluate your business or if you would like to know more about me and my company, please write or call.

OR

I will take the liberty of calling you to explain our services more fully and to learn whether you might have an interest in a price evaluation of your business.

Yours truly,

Christopher Cronin

Figure 4–5. Sample Letter for Company Owners—Version 2

(If you get the name, ask to speak to him or her. If you are asked to give your reason for calling, continue.)

"Bob, my company and I help people buy and sell businesses. We have some people interested in buying a lumberyard in this area, and I thought the owner of Steck's might know if any are for sale. I'm sure the owner would be interested in hearing about my buyers' plans."

(If you are still refused the name, continue.)

"Say, I can understand the owner's desire to keep a low profile. But, would you do this, please, Bob? Would you give the owner my name and phone number and explain that I have people looking for lumberyards and I would really appreciate some advice. The name is Chris Cronin and the number is (813) 555-1641."

"Thanks for your help, Bob."

(Optional)

"I'd like to call you later to find out the owner's reaction. Thank you. Good-bye."

Certain modifications are required when you are told that the owner is out or unavailable. Emphasize to the person on the other end of the line that it is important to the owner to know that someone interested in buying lumberyards is seeking advice. If you are just starting your activities and do not have any potential buyers yet, build your telephone script around Figure 4–5, which offers you price evaluation service, or around the idea that you just want to come by and introduce yourself. When you do get a business owner on the telephone, the objective is simply to get an appointment.

Personal contact or *canvassing* is the most time-consuming direct-marketing technique for farming but also the most powerful. Personal contact makes a stronger impression. Your physical presence emphasizes your determination. Meeting a prospective client face to face allows you to do a better job of establishing rapport and getting your message across.

Prepare for personal contact by taking along several copies of your objectives and background summary. Business cards are a must. The messages for personal contact are variations of your direct-mail letters. If you are making cold canvassing calls on businesses, the telephone script becomes your message.

Executing the Search

The targeted direct-marketing portion of your active search is now ready to go. You have your list of contacts, your messages, and their style of presentation. Lay out a timetable that permits you to stay in control. If you are using typing or mailing services, set their schedules. If you plan to do cold calls, that is, canvassing without an appointment, plan on doing a lot of call backs to contact the people who will not or cannot meet with you when you make your call. Your call back can be another personal visit or a contact by mail or telephone. If you cannot make the personal contact, do the next best thing and try to get your printed material to the targeted contact. The key to success in executing your direct-marketing program is to turn every contact into a link that will connect you eventually to a business you can list.

ADVERTISING

The advertising portion of your farming is by its nature more passive than the direct marketing. It is based on reaching the right people with the right message so that *they* will contact *you*.

The right people to target with advertising are business owners, business brokers, and other intermediaries. It is unlikely that any of the other contacts discussed would take action on your advertisement. Have decided who the right people are, you must determine the best method for reaching them. While other media may seem tempting, generally speaking, print advertising is the best method for reaching your targets.

Print Advertising

Newspapers are the best way to reach brokers and intermediaries, who regularly read the Business Opportunities section of newspapers. Which newspapers you use will depend on the business you are seeking. If you are farming small or locally oriented businesses, the local newspaper may be all you need. If the businesses are large or specialized, you may want to add the *Wall Street Journal* or one of the specialized business opportunity newspapers (see the Resources Literature section at the back of this book).

Newspaper classified advertising will be seen by business owners who read the business opportunities, but those are a small percentage of the owners you want to reach. Deciding where to advertise to reach business owners takes some analysis of what they read. Trade papers and magazines are good prospects. If the targeted businesses have a special focus, such as sports, you may want to use that section of your local newspaper.

If the businesses you want have no trade publications or special focus, accept the fact that advertising will be useful only with intermediaries. After you select the publications you are going to use, call to find out the procedures and rates for advertising. The next step is to write the advertisement based on the rate information you have obtained and the message you want to send. The objective of your ad is to get a response from your target. By putting yourself in your targets' shoes, you can easily discover what type of message would trigger that response:

1. You represent financially able buyers.

2. You are qualified.

3. You offer some service the readers want.

Here are three sample advertisements of average length. The first assumes you are farming a specific kind of business:

Wanted to Buy Lumberyard/Building Center

We represent qualified buyer(s) seeking lumberyards, garden centers, or similar businesses in Tampa/St. Petersburg. Buyers have cash. Our experience can help structure deal to meet seller's objectives. Replies held strictly confidential. C. Cronin, Statewide Agency, (813) 555-1641.

The second ad assumes you are farming a geographic area:

Businesses Wanted to Buy

We represent qualified buyers seeking businesses in the Tampa/St. Petersburg area. Price ranges up to $_____. Buyers have cash. Our experience can help structure deal to meet seller's objectives. Replies held strictly confidential. C. Cronin, Statewide Agency, (813) 555-1641.

The third ad assumes you are offering a free price evaluation:

How Much is Your Business Worth?

Do you know how much someone would pay for your business? We offer a free price evaluation based on today's market factors. All information will be held in strictest confidence. No obligation. C. Cronin, Statewide Realty, (813) 555-1641.

You will need to run your ads several times. Some owners will need to see the ad a few times to let the idea of selling develop before they will take the action of calling you. Every response generated by your farming activities needs to be evaluated and followed through. If a lead or candidate is generated that is outside your criteria, thank the source, and encourage more appropriate leads.

Seller Seminars

If your market is large enough, you may want to consider staging seminars that would provide useful information to sellers. The seminar can be designed to address common concerns of business owners, such as:

Valuing (pricing) a business

Taxes

The economic outlook

Legal considerations in selling a business

Estate considerations

Common problems

The program should be tight and well organized in consideration of the business owners' schedules. Evening programs work well in some cases. Recruit experts in each field to participate as seminar panelists. Lawyers and accountants are looking for ways to develop clients, and such a seminar could fit into their strategy. Coax business owners into attending by advertising or mailing invitations. You may not get a new listing immediately, but you have created an image of helpful professionalism. You, the accountant, and the attorney now have met a number of business owners who will become the focus of future contacts for business development.

Follow-up and Evaluation

Follow up on *every* lead you get from the active search, the seminars, and your advertising. Even if the lead is a poor one, it may be a connection to one that is worthwhile. Another reason for following up on all leads is to reinforce your reputation as a competent business person. Evaluate your farming prospects. If they are within your criteria, set up an information file and a schedule of contacts. A "Company Profile Data Form," to help you organize key information about each company you are entering in your pool, is shown as Appendix C.

A DISADVANTAGE OF THE ACTIVE SEARCH

One disadvantage of the active search, when compared to reading FSBO advertisements or talking with other brokers, is that it brings you into contact with business owners who do not want to sell but who are curious about what their business is worth. You may hear the expression, "Every business is for sale if the price is high enough." (A detailed response to this and other common issues is presented later in this chapter.) You can waste a lot of time with these owners unless you quickly determine whether they are potential sellers. Ask for the selling price and say that, in order to know whether that price is fair, you need to see the financial records. If you are asked to offer a price evaluation, point out that you are more than willing to do so but you will, of course, need to see the financial records. And of course, you may decide to charge for evaluations. If the owner refuses to let you see the books, you can either ask him or her for an alternative way to proceed or you can assume the seller is not serious and move on to other businesses.

You have generated your pool of candidate companies. You have identified sources and contacts, developed lists of contact names, and implemented an active search. You have used direct marketing techniques, seminars, and advertising to build your farming network. (Worksheet 2 at the end of this chapter and Figure 4–1 will help you organize your efforts.) Now that your telephone has begun to ring, where do you focus your effort next? We will move on now to the task of converting these potential sellers into listings.

THE LISTING MEETING AND PRESENTATION

What follows is an idealized version of the listing meeting and presentation. You know from your real estate experience that things will not go perfectly. You will have to apply all your skills and remain very flexible in actual listing situations.

THE APPOINTMENT

Pick a time and place that best suits the purpose of the meeting. Confidentiality and convenience are important considerations. Unless you know the business well or there is some compelling objection, meet on the business premises. Help the seller set his or her expectations when you make your appointment. Tell the seller you would like to see the business as part of your visit. Ask the seller to prepare for the meeting. If the rapport is strong enough, ask that he or she have the following available at the meeting:

1. Three to five years' financial statements
2. Tax returns for the same period
3. A copy of the lease
4. Samples of company literature, advertising, etc.
5. A list of equipment, if relevant

If you feel the seller is willing to do so at this early stage, you might ask how long the business has been in operation, the number of employees, and the approximate sales volume. Don't press too hard for this information at this point. Getting the appointment is the important objective.

YOUR OBJECTIVES

The first three objectives of the listing meeting for businesses are the same as for real estate:

1. Understand the seller, the property, and the seller's desires.
2. Present yourself and your firm's qualifications favorably.
3. Get the listing.

The procedure requires much more in the way of information gathering, however, because there is a fourth objective:

4. Obtain enough information to be able to market the business.

MEETING PREPARATION

It is a sign of your professionalism and your interest in the seller to show up for your listing meeting well prepared and well informed. Never assume you have the listing. Being overly casual and underprepared can cost you the seller's confidence and the listing.

Before your appointment, learn as much as you can about the business and the seller. You must do your fact finding as discreetly as possible, of course. Asking too many questions too obviously could cause people to suspect your motives. After all, you will get the chance to ask the seller eventually. It is a real plus, however, to know in advance:

- What the business does
- How long it has been in business
- The reputation of the business (and the owner)
- The real estate facts, if relevant

If the business is a restaurant, eat there. If it's a retail store, shop there. Go to the Yellow Pages and take a look at the competition. If you know someone in the same business, ask a few questions, but remember: Be discreet.

What you can assemble in the way of written promotional material for your business will, of course, depend on what you have. At a minimum, you should have a summary of your own background and qualifications. A company brochure describing your services is a common tool. Samples of advertising and direct-mail campaigns are concrete examples that can help strengthen your points. The seller wants to know what your marketing and selling programs are. Testimonials or announcements of past successful transactions are good support pieces.

Obviously, you want to take along your listing agreements for both businesses and real estate (if you have them separately). The many unique details of a business listing usually result in a false start, so be sure you have extra listing forms. You will find a sample of an "Exclusive Right to Sell" listing agreement as Appendix A at the back of this book.

A good device to reinforce your claim of professionalism is a "Confidential Receipt of Information" form. This is the form that prospective buyers must sign before they receive any information. The form should also provide a disclaimer of any warranties on the information being provided to the prospective buyer. A sample of a "Confidential Receipt of Information" form appears as Appendix B. Sellers are concerned about confidentiality, and providing the form during your presentation can be an excellent way to earn their confidence.

The "Offer to Purchase" form, shown as Appendix G, is a good listing tool because it focuses your presentation on the seller's main concern—the actual sale. Presenting the offer form serves another purpose. It allows you to prepare the seller for the realities of how offers are likely to be made. It gives you the chance to talk about contingencies and due diligence (both of which will be covered in Chapter 11) and the other variations that typically make up an offer on a business. If you have buyers on file for that type of business, bring their profiles along. You need not show their names to the seller; just show the existence of real potential buyers whom you could quickly bring forward.

THE PRESENTATION

Presentation style is a personal issue. The presentation proposed here is merely a guide that you can adapt to your own style. It is also intended to encourage a high degree of flexibility in how each phase is executed.

After the introductions and salutations, your first step is to get the seller's permission to set the procedure for the presentation. Ideally, you want to *learn* about the seller and the business, *explain* your capabilities, and *agree* on how to go forward. You can begin by suggesting that agenda to the seller.

Learn About the Seller and the Business

There are two questions that can help you meet this objective:

1. "How and when did you get into this business?"
2. "Why are you considering selling?"

One piece of information you need more than any other is the owner's reason for selling. It can be an important clue to the condition of the business. Unfortunately, as we mentioned in Chapter 1, you may get acceptable-sounding answers such as "I have other business interests," or "I'm retiring," when the real reason is "I can't hire any help," or "Competition is killing me." Probe carefully any reason you are given. Ask to know more about the other business interests or the retirement. You may have to use several different approaches in order to learn about the owner's future plans. The opening questions are designed to get you into the topic. Your direction after that will be governed by the answers you receive, the importance of this factor to the particular company, and the seller's willingness and ability to share information. (You may be better off getting some of the answers from others or from your own observation.)

The basic plan for obtaining company information is merely to work your way down a list of business factors and ask questions.

Figure 4–6 is a summary of the information you will need. Table 4–1 lists some opening questions.

Many more questions can, and will, be generated as you actually dig out the information. Don't be surprised if the seller cannot answer all of them. Some of this information is facts that are not kept handy; some questions will not be understood; and some are not factors internal to the business.

When you and a buyer are ready to analyze the business (Chapter 9), you will find in Figure 9–2 over 30 sources of information about the business in addition to the seller. As a reminder, keep the information organized with the Company Profile Data Form (see Appendix C).

Explain Your Capabilities

The owner must have confidence in your ability to sell the business. You need to demonstrate your understanding of the business, present your experience, describe your resources, and outline your plan for marketing the business. Offer to recap the major features of the business and the owner's stated reason for selling as a way to show that you have gained an understanding. Recapping can also serve

> The owner's reason for selling
> Company history
> The company's purpose, what it does
> People
> Organization
> Facilities
> Equipment
> Technology
> Market
> Competition
> Company operations:
>   Manufacturing
>   Legal
>   Marketing and sales
>   Accounting and finance
> General strengths and weaknesses
> Outside factors
> Financial performance

Figure 4–6. What Information Is Needed

TABLE 4–1   Sample Opening Questions

Business Factor	Opening Questions
History	When and how did the company start? What has been its history of ownership and activity? Who owns the company now, and in what form is the ownership?
Purpose	What is the fundamental nature of the business? What does it do? Why does it exist? Does it have a plan or direction?
People	Who are they? How many are there? How long have they been there? What do they do? Are they competent? Are they satisfied? Are any of them critical to success? Is there a union? How well are they paid? Are there enough of them? Is there a manager other than the owner? Will key people leave if a sale takes place?
Organization	What is it? Does it work well? What function does the owner play? Are there organizational policies and practices? Is there depth in the organization?
Facilities (Plant or Office)	What are they? Is the size right? Own or rent? What are the terms and length of the lease? Is it assumable? Is the facility where it should be? What is the condition of the facility? What would it take to relocate?
Equipment	What is it? Is it modern? Is it well kept? What is the percent utilization? Is there enough/not enough? Who supplies it? Who maintains it? Could it be easily sold?
Technology	Are company methods and techniques modern? Are products and services modern? How does the company provide for innovation? Does technology change rapidly? What computer system does the company use?
Market	What/who is the company's market? How large is it? Is it growing or declining? Is it concentrated on a few customers or spread broadly? Is it style- or fad-based?
Competition	Who are the competitors? Is competition increasing? Do competitors have any special advantages? Who has what share of the market, and how is that changing? Are any competitors for sale?

Company Operations: (as appropriate)

Manufacturing	What is the manufacturing process? What is the total capacity? How much is available? What would it cost to expand? How is productivity measured? Any special skills required? Any special dependence on suppliers? Any problems with EPA? Any labor problems?
Legal	Is the company involved in litigation? Is there some exposure? What contracts or obligations does the company have? Who is the company's attorney? Does the company require licenses to operate, or is it otherwise regulated? Does it have any patents? To what associations does the company belong? Does the company have adequate insurance?
Marketing and Sales	What are the key marketing activities and techniques? How many people do what tasks? How are the products and services perceived in the marketplace? What have been the trends in sales volume and prices? How are prices set? How are sales people hired, trained, and compensated?

	How many customers does the company have? Are sales concentrated among a few customers? How geographically spread out are the customers? Has the company lost any customers? Are customers long established? Do they sign contracts? Will they stay on after the sale?
Accounting/Finance	How is the accounting and/or financial function organized? Is it adequate for the company's needs? Are systems and reports satisfactory? Who is the company's outside accountant? Who is the company's banker? Are adequate lines of credit established? Does the company pay its bills on a schedule?
General	What are the strengths and weaknesses of the company? What area needs the most immediate improvement? Where does the company's greatest potential lie? What is the biggest threat to the company?
Outside Factors	Are there any special problems or opportunities relating to general economic conditions, world trade, governmental agencies, or other outside factors?
Financial Performance (Before asking the questions, determine if the information you have is complete and accurate. Get 3 to 5 years of figures if you can.)	Is the company profitable? How profitable? Is it growing? Is enough cash being generated to operate the business? What adjustments are needed to get from the accountant's profit to the owner's cash flow? Study trends.
Balance Sheet	What has been the trend of inventory? How much is finished goods, how much is raw material, how much is work in progress? Is the inventory worth the value? Has the level of accounts receivable varied? How old are they? Are they owed by a few or many customers? What are the fixed and other assets? How have fixed assets been valued and depreciated? What market value do they have? Has the level of accounts payable varied? To whom are they owed? Are they current? Identify the debt and each creditor. How much is it? What is the trend? How old is it?
Income (P&L) Statement	What have been the trends in sales? In costs? Have any expense items changed significantly? Is adequate money being spent on repairs (or any other item)?
Ratios	If you can, set up the following ratios/percentages: Return on Investment, Return on Sales, Individual Expense Items to Sales, Costs to Sales, Current Assets to Current Liabilities, Income (Cash) to Debt Payments, Receivable Turns per Year, Inventory Turns per Year, Salaries and Benefits as a Percentage of Total Expenses. (There will be further discussion on ratios later in the chapter.)

to verify the facts. If you or your firm have business brokerage experience, tell the owner about some of your past sales. Present references if you can. If you and your firm are new, describe your real estate background and explain how it is relevant. Talk about your personal qualifications: certifications, education, training, awards, and so on. Mention the clubs and networks to which you belong. If you have some special connection with the type of business, such as a relative in the business or a lifelong interest in the field, say so. If you are a member of a large, active firm with high visibility, attractive literature, sophisticated systems, plenty of financial backing, and professional management, you have a lot to describe. But if you have few or none of the above, you still have one resource that is the most valuable to the seller—your time and ingenuity. You can explain that selling businesses requires much less general or organizational effort and much more personal effort.

Most people know what a real estate salesperson can do to help sell a house. Few people know what a business broker can do. Explain that you can provide the following services, leaving the owner free to run the business:

1. **Pricing**. Done without the owner's bias or the accountant's conventions, but rather from the point of view of the buyer—the only real market authority on price.

2. **Packaging**. Preparing a written description of the business and its functions. That often involves restating the financial aspects in a more relevant form (removing extra benefits).

3. **Marketing**. Using appropriate techniques, from general advertising to personal contacts.

4. **Screening**. Qualifying buyers to save time and to maintain confidentiality.

5. **Selling**. Selling a business is itself a skill that involves identifying the needs, presenting the benefits, overcoming the objections, and getting the offer.

6. **Negotiations**. The complexity of a business sale requires negotiation on many points, such as terms, closing dates, and assignment of values.

7. **Financing**. A buyer can be helped in finding sources of money to complete the transaction.

8. **Other assistance**. Obtaining appraisals, assisting in licensing and making closing arrangements.

The final demonstration of your capabilities is to provide the seller with an idea of what you plan to do. You don't have enough information to give a detailed marketing and sales plan yet. And you shouldn't give one, because the seller may then feel he or she has enough information to sell the business without you. Your description of your plan can mention key marketing elements, such as advertising and direct mail. Show examples of marketing and sales programs you have done. Sample advertisements and mail pieces can help. Stress your personal networking. If you have a pool of buyers, explain how you will use them. Much of your plan will depend on who the most likely buyers are. You will need to develop a profile of the typical buyer and decide how best to find him or her. (Chapter 5 is devoted to finding buyers.) From the beginning, involve the seller in the business selling process. You will need the help and will benefit from the team relationship.

Agree on How to Go Forward

This is the most complex step of the listing presentation. In a real estate setting, one would typically press for a signature on a listing agreement and, once gained, talk about the calendar of events for advertising, open house, and so on. The business listing involves some issues that make such a straightforward procedure unlikely:

- *Pricing*—The first issue is really a dilemma. In the previous chapter, the techniques for pricing a business were discussed. You will recall that they are involved and require considerable analysis to perform. You will want to take the financial figures and analyze them in depth in your office, which means you cannot put a price into the listing agreement while you are at your listing meeting. A further dilemma with price arises over who suggests the selling price first—you or the seller. If the seller does it, the plus is that you know what the initial expectations are. The minus is that you may now have an extremely difficult time moving the seller off that price if it is unrealistic. If you suggest the price first, you will have a starting point you feel is proper, but you may turn the prospective seller off if the figure is far from what he or she has in mind.

- *Signing the listing*—This issue has proponents and opponents. Some brokers feel the listing should be signed, just as in real estate, at the conclusion of the listing meeting. These brokers do not want to risk the seller changing his or her mind or deciding to go FSBO. They will reach some agreement on price even if it means accepting the seller's price. What these brokers do is to inform the seller that they will review the price and be back to discuss revisions. Other brokers take a nearly opposite approach. They view the process as complicated and unique enough to warrant two meetings. They leave a listing form, which is much more complicated than a real estate form (see Appendix A, "Exclusive Right to Sell" form), for the owner to review and take a day or two to develop a price. They then return with a completed form ready for signature.

One other important issue exists in business sales. If a company sells all or substantially all of its assets outside the normal course of its business, most states require the board of directors and, under some conditions, the stockholders, to approve such a sale. You should receive a corporate resolution authorizing the sale. If you are in doubt, ask your own attorney.

- *Setting expectations*—If you haven't already done so, explain the process of selling a business to the seller. Discuss the steps and the time it can take. Describe how buyers act and how they typically go about examining a business for sale. If the seller hasn't considered them, discuss the terms of sale and why he or she might have to help the buyer finance the purchase. Review how and how often you will update the seller on the progress of your activities. If the business or its records need to be put in better shape, tactfully explain what is needed and why. You may also want to prepare the seller for a common phenomenon in business sales. Often, when a business first comes on the market, there is immediate and serious interest from one or several potential buyers. The seller wrongly concludes that selling will be easy and that he or she should hold out and wait for even better prospects. Inform the seller that these conclusions are wrong. Strong early activity means there was someone searching or waiting for this kind of business. If the seller squanders these seemingly easy-to-get buyer candidates, he or she may wait a long time until you are able to build enough interest to attract the next candidates.

Finally, prepare the seller for the complexities of the transactions. One way is to give the seller a copy of the "Closing Checklist" (see Chapter 11, Figure 11–2). All in all, you want the seller as a satisfied client and an active partner in the sale.

Your style, the nature and size of the business, and the attitude of the seller will all influence how you handle these special issues.

COLD-CALL CANVASSING FOR LISTINGS

For many years, knocking on business doors was the primary technique for getting listings. It can still be effective, particularly with businesses that are accessible to the public, such as retail stores and restaurants.

YOUR OBJECTIVES

The ultimate objective is still the same—you want the listing. Of course, you also want to create a good and memorable impression and learn as much as you can. It is realistic to assume you are less likely to get a listing from a cold call than you are from an appointment. That fact leads some brokers to use cold canvassing primarily as a means to get a scheduled listing meeting. In any event, almost every cold call can and should become part of your listing farm.

CALL PREPARATION

Much of the preparation for a cold call is the same as for a listing meeting:

- Background on the business—Probably even more important on the cold call so that you create an image of a professional rather than a door-to-door solicitor. Getting the background is time-consuming, but, remember, you haven't had to do the other farming work.

- Written promotional material—This may be all you get to use, so it is important.

- Your forms and agreements—You want to be able to take a listing on the spot, so you will need them.

- Buyers on file—This is the cornerstone of cold-call canvassing. It is the best reason you can give for taking the owner's time.

- Scheduling the meeting—Instead of setting a meeting time, you will need to plan your calls so that you have the best chance of being able to spend time with the owner. Avoid peak times when the owner is involved and busy.

THE PRESENTATION

The essence of the cold-call listing presentation is to convey to owners that you are in regular contact with people who are interested in buying businesses like theirs. An often-used approach follows a script like this:

> "Mr. Smith, my name is Tom East. My company and I help people buy and sell businesses. I have not heard that you are for sale, but we have buyers looking for (your type) business, and I thought I'd stop and ask."

A follow-up element of the cold call sounds like this:

> "May I take just a minute to tell you what we can do to help sellers?"

Here you would present your services.

No exact script can be written, but you will, with practice, be able to cover all the elements in a regular listing meeting: *learning* about the business, *explaining* your capabilities, and *agreeing* on the next steps. You may be asked to come back at a time more convenient to the owner. You then have a regular listing appointment. The same issues of pricing and signing the listing apply to the cold call as they did to the listing meeting.

COMMON SITUATIONS

Whether you are conducting cold calls or scheduled meetings, be prepared to encounter certain attitudes on a regular basis.

"ANY BUSINESS IS FOR SALE AT SOME PRICE"

Business owners often use that pricing cliche jokingly, but with some seriousness. Almost every business owner would like to know what someone would pay for his or her business. You can use this curiosity four ways.

Use Free Price Evaluations to Get Listing Appointments

Offering free price evaluations is an almost sure way to get listing appointments. The question is whether the percentage of free evaluations you convert to listings is worth your time. To someone just starting out to list and sell businesses, it is probably a good use of time and an excellent way to gain experience.

Rebate the Fee for Price Evaluations

Under this strategy, you set a fee for conducting a price evaluation but agree to rebate the fee under certain conditions. The most generous condition is to rebate the fee if you are given the listing. A less generous but common alternative is to credit the fee against any commission owed on a sale.

Use Price Evaluations to Earn Fee Income

Here is a way to generate income that is unique to business opportunities. Because of the complexity involved in conducting a price evaluation, charging a fee is acceptable. It is fair, and it recognizes value and effort. There are outside services that business brokers can use to process price evaluations. Business Evaluation Systems*, for example, offers four different price evaluation programs that brokers can either purchase or use on a per case basis. Some brokers use services like this to process their price evaluations and then mark up the fee to cover the time and effort they spent gathering, organizing, and interpreting the data.

Use Price Evaluations to Improve the Quality of a Listing

Two positive things happen when you conduct a formal price evaluation. First, the seller has had to produce the facts and figures on the business. This is not always an easy thing to get the seller to do. Second, you have been able to apply the best thinking available to reach a fair and marketable price. This puts you in a much better position than using the seller's top-of-the-head asking price or a price you have had to generate quickly or on bits and pieces of information.

---

*Business Evaluation Systems, Box 50074, Houston, TX 77250

"BRING ME A BUYER AND WE'LL TALK"

This is more commonly heard in cold-call situations, but is not uncommon in any listing meeting. Your approach and your options are again similar to those you have in real estate.

Get the Information Necessary to List and Sell the Business

The old standby response goes roughly like this:

> "I'd be glad to bring you a buyer, Mr. Smith. Now, in order for me to determine if my buyer(s) would be interested and appropriate, I'll need a few facts."

Try to Convert the Opening Into a Standard Listing

Your sales abilities may be what will convince a genuine seller to take the next step and agree to a standard listing. Your best argument is that, while you do have an interested buyer, you may be able to bring even better buyers forward once you begin to actively seek them. In order to spend that time and money, of course, you need and deserve a listing.

Accept the "One by One" Listing

This type of listing is not uncommon in business opportunity sales. (Exclusive agency and open listings are also used.) The first time you do bring a buyer in to see the business, you will uncover much of the information you need to determine if the business and the seller are worth your time.

Reject or Postpone the Listing

You always have this option, and, many times, it is the right one. Some business owners love the attention and the chance to talk about their businesses. They can take up just as much or even more time than the serious seller. Naturally, you do want to leave the owner with a positive impression, and you should follow up in case he or she does become serious.

"I WON'T PAY YOUR HIGH COMMISSION"

If you have been able to present the full menu of services you are planning to provide and have explained your qualifications, you can defend your right to a commission.

The Amount of the Commission

If the issue is the amount of the commission, you may need to restate the effort and resources you are prepared to expend. If you are competitive with other business opportunity sellers, say so. Find out what specific objections the seller has and try to combat them. Tell the seller that by using you, he or she will save more than the amount of your commission in the number of valuable owner hours freed up to devote to the business.

Commissions are, in fact, negotiable. Commissions of 10 to 12 percent, with minimum commissions ranging from $6,000 to $10,000, are common. For larger businesses, the so-called Lehman formula is used:

5% on the first $1 million in sales price plus

4% "   second   "

3% "   third   "

2% "   fourth   "

1% on anything over $4 million in sales price.

Under the Lehman formula, a business that sells for $5 million generates a total commission of $150,000 (3%). A $10 million sale produces a $200,000 commission (2%), and so on.

Commissions are sometimes paid over a period of time. If the seller is receiving only half the price at closing and the other half over the next five years, you may be asked to take your commission in a corresponding arrangement. The terms and security of such a payment may well be acceptable to you, particularly if it is what allows a transaction to come together. Custom, market conditions, and your philosophy will shape your approach to this (always present) fact of any brokerage business.

The Objection to Any Commission

Some owners will simply say, "You can bring buyers forward, but they have to pay the commission." Buyer–broker arrangements, where the buyer agrees to pay the commission, are not uncommon. They are covered in Chapter 6 and may well fit some situations. It is difficult to convince a buyer to pay the commission, but he or she is really paying it in any event. The economic logic is that the seller has in mind a net price objective. Whether the commission is added to that price and paid by the seller or left off and paid by the buyer, the result is theoretically the same. The buyer also has a net price in mind and views the commission as a part of the cost of buying the business. The price and the commission become one total in the buyer's analysis of the purchase.

The final issue involves the concept and duties of agency. If the seller can be made to understand that the commission has, taxes ignored, the same economic impact no matter who pays it, then the only difference becomes determining for whom the broker is working. If the seller insists that the buyer pay the commission, then the buyer will have to engage the broker and the broker will owe his or her loyalty to the buyer. If you are successful in conveying this fact and in selling your value, you may convince the seller to pay your commission.

"I WANT ALL CASH OR NO SALE"

Many sellers start from the position that only an all-cash sale will meet their needs. As you would in any situation, find out the reasons for the need and respond to them. There are several points you can make.

It Makes it Harder to Sell the Business

Banks and other conventional lending sources usually want assets as security. Most small businesses, particularly service businesses, have few assets. That means the buyer has to have enough wealth to put up all the money, a fact that narrows the market, sometimes so much that no one will or can buy the business.

This Owner is in Competition with Other Business Sellers

If most other businesses are offered for sale with a 25 to 50 percent downpayment, it means that the buyer has a chance to buy a much larger business for the same initial cash outlay.

Terms Affect Price

You know from any exposure to mortgage tables that financing affects the buyer's ability to pay. You also know that a property is easier to sell if the financing is available and attractive. The same applies to businesses. An all-cash price may be very acceptable if it is a lower alternative to a higher price financed by seller's terms.

Buyers Can Provide Security

The seller who worries about the buyer's ability to repay can seek security. The business itself might become the security. The buyer's real estate or personal guarantee are other forms that can be used.

DESIRE, INTEREST, AND ENTHUSIASM

Finally, nothing can tip the scales in your favor to get the listing like convincing the owner you are excited about the business and you truly want to help him or her sell it. The owner of the business usually views that business in deeply personal terms. It's not like a house that someone can duplicate. It is one of a kind, and the owner will want a broke who can understand and appreciate its uniqueness. And, of course, the owner wants someone who will work hard to sell the business. Successful business owners are themselves hard working and will want to feel their agent will also work hard. Listing and selling businesses truly is hard work, so all you will need to do is develop a means of communicating that you are prepared to do whatever it takes to help your client sell the business.

WORKSHEET 2

Sources & Contacts for Locating the Business

Source	Specific Contact Comments
Newspapers	_____
Newsletters	_____
Trade magazines	_____
Business brokers	_____
Business owners	_____
Other business people	_____
Lawyers, accountants, other advisors	_____
Bankers and investment bankers	_____
Venture capitalists, merger and acquisition specialists, corporate development executives	_____
Networks	_____
Vendors and suppliers	_____
Customers	_____
Industry trade associations	_____
Others	_____

CHAPTER 5

Finding Buyers

There are two unique aspects to finding business buyers. The first has to do with the specialized activities involved in finding buyers for a specific business. The second relates to the need to find and manage a pool of general business buyers.

FINDING BUYERS FOR SPECIFIC BUSINESSES

Identifying these buyers is a classic marketing challenge. You need to know whom to reach, where they can be found, how best to reach them, and how to elicit their response.

PROFILING THE INDIVIDUAL BUYER

When you are seeking individual buyers for a specific business, begin by developing profiles of those most likely to buy this business. Define the knowledge, skills, and other traits or characteristics that the perfect buyer would possess. This about the financial resources of your perfect buyer. Your seller can be your best source of help in developing this profile, but be careful that the seller's ego doesn't define some superior being who is impossible to find or that the seller's eagerness to sell doesn't define everyone with enough money.

Knowledge

What does a person need *to know* to successfully operate this business? Here are some categories of knowledge for you to consider:

- Industry knowledge
- Community knowledge
- Business practices knowledge
- Technical or specialized knowledge

Skills

What *types of skills* does a person need to be successful in this business? Here are some examples of skills:

- Selling skills
- Administrative skills
- People management skills
- Negotiating skills
- Technical or specialized skills

Traits and Characteristics

Defining *what the buyer will be like* is less simple, but more critical to profiling the perfect buyer successfully:

- Personal and physical traits—Does the buyer need a special level of strength or stamina, or will a "couch potato" do?
- Proclivities—What are the likes and dislikes of the perfect buyer? If given a choice, how would the buyer spend his or her time?
- Special traits—Would the perfect buyer have some creative, athletic, or other talent? Would he or she have (or not have) some special social characteristics or some particular risk profile?

There is a curious aspect to dealing with buyers. Some of them are motivated by a strong desire to escape from or change their situations. They will pay little attention to their knowledge, skills, and traits. They simply *want a business*. Knowledge, skills, and traits will be examined from the buyer's perspective in Chapter 6.

Financial Resources

Because you are looking for buyers for a specific business, you know the price and terms, so you know the buyer's profile in this regard.

PROFILING ANOTHER COMPANY AS THE BUYER

Often the best buyer for your specific business listing is another company. Companies regularly look to absorb competition, expand geographically, or otherwise obtain special economic advantages by acquiring other companies. Profile these corporate buyers by examining their objectives and motives.

Competitors

These are relatively easy to profile. The Yellow Pages, industry directories, and the seller can all provide names and addresses of competitive firms. The seller can help you eliminate those that are not appropriate because of size, reputation, or other factors. Competitors are not necessarily the best buyers. Often they only want part of the business, such as the customers or the employees, and so will pay less. Letting competitors know that the business is for sale is risky because they may cause problems with customers and others. Also, letting competitors see the business close up can give them all they need to gain an advantage.

Companies Seeking Geographic Expansion

Companies in the same or similar fields as your listed business that are located in other markets may be looking to expand into your area. In order to gain the interest of a distant company, your listing must include some particularly desired feature and/or the distant company must already have an interest in expanding into your area.

Companies Seeking Some Special Economic or Strategic Advantage

It takes some creativity, but you should be able to identify other companies as possible buyer candidates. The key is knowing what

special assets and features your listed company has and then identifying who would benefit most from owning them. Here are examples
of some economic features that might benefit another company:

- High earnings
- Trained employees
- A special location
- A hard-to-obtain license or franchise
- A source of a needed raw material or component
- A valuable customer list or market position
- A unique technology
- A favorable lease
- A backlog of business/contracts
- Valuable assets, such as machinery, equipment, accounts re-
  ceivable
- A recognized company name and reputation

The purpose of profiling buyers, whether individuals or companies, is to determine who the best candidates are. The next step
is knowing where to find them.

LOCATING BUYERS

Where you will look for buyers will depend on how narrowly or
broadly you were able to develop your profile. If your profile of the
perfect buyer contains no special requirements in knowledge, skills,
or traits, you have a very broad population from which to choose,
and buyers should be everywhere. If, on the other hand, your buyer
needs some special experience in, say, restaurant operations, he or
she will be located in or around the restaurant industry. Buyers for
small mom and pop operations will be found locally. Deciding where
to find buyers is a common-sense task.

REACHING BUYERS

You will use a different mix of marketing techniques in selling
businesses than is used in selling real estate. Some of the everyday

mainstays of real estate marketing are not appropriate for businesses. Both the open house and the use of multiple listings eliminate confidentiality by revealing the identity of the business. They are rarely used. Currently, promoting to other brokers is also not a common practice.

Just as you did with potential sellers, you will need some marketing tools to use in your contacts with potential buyers. A *brochure* describing your firm and its services was mentioned earlier as a listing tool. It can serve as a sales tool as well (see Appendix D for a sample sales brochure). A *personal promotion sheet* may be appropriate to present your background and qualifications (see Appendix E). A *Confidential Receipt of Information* form is used to reinforce the requirement for confidentiality. The form, shown as Appendix B, accomplishes several things:

- The buyer acknowledges receipt of specific confidential information.
- The buyer agrees to maintain confidentiality.
- The buyer recognizes the broker as the procuring broker.
- The buyer acknowledges the broker's disclaimer of responsibility for the accuracy or completeness of any information presented.
- The buyer agrees to conduct his or her own due diligence investigation.

Fact sheets and write-ups on each business are a must. There are many styles of write-ups. Larger and more complex businesses will require more complex write-ups; smaller businesses need only brief fact sheets. Figure 5–1 is an example of a basic fact sheet. The form contains all the pertinent facts and can be used to conduct initial discussions. The name of the business is not revealed until the buyer expresses interest in knowing more and agrees to sign the confidentiality form. Figure 5–2 is an example of a more narrative, persuasive selling sheet. Unlike in the real estate market, photographs are seldom used. Not only would they destroy confidentiality, but most businesses are not eye-pleasing subjects. More complete write-ups, often called *packages*, might contain:

- Financial statements
- Equipment lists
- Tax returns

```
┌──────────────────────────────────────────────────────────────────────────┐
│                         BUSINESS PROFILE              FILE NO. C 326        │
│   BUSINESS NAME        (confidential) _____            │
│                                                                            │
│   ADDRESS              _____                 │
│                                                                            │
│   CONTACT PH#          _____                 │
│                                                                            │
│   TYPE OF BUSINESS     1 hour photo processing    _____                │
│                                                                            │
│                        EST.  1979                                          │
│                        PRESENT OWNER SINCE      1979                        │
│                                                                            │
│   ORGANIZATION CORP. x     PARTNERSHIP __    SOLE PROPRIETOR __             │
│                                                                            │
│   NO. OF EMPLOYEES 2 FT 2 PT     UNION __     NON UNION  X                  │
│                                                                            │
│   AVERAGE WAGE OF EMPLOYEE PER HR.   $7.00                                  │
│                                                                            │
│   DAYS OF OPERATION 6–closed Sunday   HOURS OF OPERATION 9–6:30             │
│                                                                            │
│   LICENSE REQUIRED  Sales Tax - City License                               │
│                                                                            │
│   BUILDINGS/SPACE SIZE     3,000 SQ. FT                                     │
│      BASE MO. RENTAL       $3,562                                           │
│      LEASE EXP. DATE       1990 option to renew for 5 years (+ CPI)         │
│                                                                            │
│   ASSETS   FURNITURE, FIXTURES, & EQUIPMENT          $133,000              │
│                                                                            │
│            LEASEHOLD IMPROVEMENT                     $ 25,000              │
│                                                                            │
│            INVENTORY     x INCLUDED IN SALE          $  5,000              │
│                                                                            │
│                          __ EXCLUDED FROM SALE                            │
│                                                                            │
│   SALES    ANNUAL GROSS SALES            1986 -      $200,000              │
│                                          1987 -      $242,000              │
│                                          1988 -      $300,000              │
│            ANNUAL OWNER INCOME                       $ 50,000              │
│                                                                            │
│   (Approx) PRICE        $225,000       TERMS NEGOTIABLE                     │
│                                                                            │
│   REASON FOR SALE  Owner retiring out of state                             │
│                                                                            │
│   REMARKS/SELLING POINTS Excellent like-new equipment. Great location with │
│                      good lease. Loyal employees. Priced for a quick sale. │
│                                                                            │
│   FINANCIAL INFORMATION HAS BEEN PROVIDED BY THE SELLER. BROKER            │
│   DOES NOT GUARANTEE ITS ACCURACY OR COMPLETENESS.                         │
└──────────────────────────────────────────────────────────────────────────┘
```

Figure 5–1. Basic Fact Sheet

$2.5 Million Electrical Fixture Manufacturer

This business is 40 years old and is located in Southern Fairfield County. Owner cash flow approximates $250,000. (Financial disclosure will be made during serious negotiations).

The nature of the business is manufacturing lighting fixtures such as those that house fluorescent lights. The fixtures are of many styles; recessed, dropped, wraparound, egg crate, and others for both commercial and residential use. The company has a manufacturing niche. It is considered medium-sized and can handle both standard and nonstandard products. It can do modifications that large automated manufacturers won't do and can produce enough product quickly, something smaller companies can't do.

The basic process involves metalworking to produce the frames, painting, assembly, and packing. The work force of 45 requires no craftsmen. The plant is unionized, and relations are good.

An equipment list is attached. The owner can show that the present plant, working one shift plus some overtime, has the capacity to produce $7 million in volume. Present sales are $2,525,000.

The plant occupies 42,000 square feet of a 46,000 square foot building that is owned by the seller. The lease will be $130,000 per year.

In addition to the equipment, there are receivables approximating $350,000 and inventory of $100,000.

There is no formal marketing and sales effort. Sales are made solely in response to inquiries.

The market consists of builders, contractors, architects, and some government business. Distributors and representatives are not used.

The asking price for the business is $1 million plus inventory (at cost). The seller will assume all payables and debt.

The seller will finance a major portion of the purchase.

The information presented here has been supplied by the seller. Broker does not guarantee its accuracy or completeness.

Figure 5–2. Narrative Selling Sheet

- A copy of the lease
- A roster of key employees
- Market statistics
- A company history
- Appraisals and evaluations
- Important contracts
- Company catalogs, brochures, and other literature
- Business plans
- Competitor analyses
- Other materials that would help sell the business

Business cards and stationery are even more important in business sales than in the real estate field because of the long length of time you may be working with potential buyers (and sellers). You need these tools to keep your name in front of these people.

Networks and Personal Contacts

It will be no surprise to the experienced real estate salesperson that personal promotion through networks, organizations, and everyday individual contacts is a key element of business sales. Because you have already determined where you will find your buyers for a specific business, you can focus your networking. An example is a restaurant listing. One of the first things you will learn is that restaurant buyers, both individuals and companies, are predominantly already in the restaurant business. Every time you go into a restaurant it is a relatively easy task to ask the owner, captain, maitre d', bartender, and anyone else you speak with, the following type of question:

> "Do you know anyone who would be interested in having a really nice, 60-seat family restaurant out near the beach? I have one for sale and could use some help finding the right buyer."

You may get plenty of information right on the spot, but you should also leave your business card, brochure, and a copy of the write-up (without the name) to encourage follow-up. Get the names of more cooperative people and build a file of them for future use.

The steps outlined here to *sell* a restaurant are going to pay off to *get listings* as well. You will become recognized as an active and knowledgeable person who employs professional techniques.

Paying for listing leads was mentioned in Chapter 4. The same issues apply to paying for sales leads. If your state laws allow it, and if it is in keeping with the tone of your market, meaningful rewards for successful leads can provide you with a large stable of referral people. In successful networking, both parties benefit. If you can't pay money for leads, you can pay in information on new listings, recent sales, and so on. If you have identified the correct networks, your information about businesses for sale will be seen as very interesting and valuable by those who receive it.

Direct Mail and Telephone Contacts

If you have an identified pool of individual buyers or if you are after companies as buyers for your listing, direct mail and telephone contacts are two extremely effective methods. Marketing people today feel it is necessary to use both mail and telephone contacts. Perhaps there is an overload of direct mail marketing, or perhaps the sale of a business is too significant an activity for just a mailing; adding telephone contact to a good mail piece seems more effective. Figure 5–3 is an example of a cover letter to be used with the business write-ups shown in Figures 5–1 and 5–2. The letter highlights several

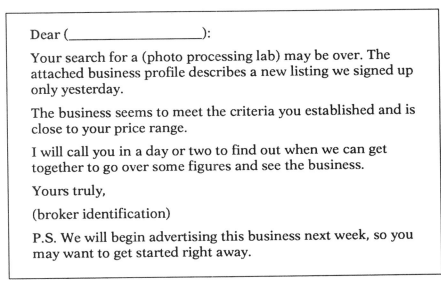

Dear (_____):

Your search for a (photo processing lab) may be over. The attached business profile describes a new listing we signed up only yesterday.

The business seems to meet the criteria you established and is close to your price range.

I will call you in a day or two to find out when we can get together to go over some figures and see the business.

Yours truly,

(broker identification)

P.S. We will begin advertising this business next week, so you may want to get started right away.

Figure 5–3. Cover Letter for Direct Mail

features of the business while maintaining confidentiality. The reader is given notice of a follow-up phone call, which will pave the way for your next contact.

Advertising a Specific Business

Print advertising is generally the most cost effective means of advertising for specific businesses. In this chapter, you have reviewed the need to know *whom* you are trying to reach and *where* you might find them. You may have concluded that perfect buyers for your specific business are not the people already in the market who are reading the "Business Opportunity" section of your local paper. To be sure, the "Business Opportunity" section of your local paper will probably be the major medium for your advertising, but it will not be the only one. For larger businesses, you may use the "Mart" section of Wednesday's or Thursday's *Wall Street Journal*. If you are trying to attract buyers with some special skill, you might use the appropriate technical publication. Company buyers for your listing might best be reached in an industry trade journal. A fitness center business might be advertised in the sports section, a boutique in the fashion section, and so on.

Once you know what your buyers read, you can tailor your advertisement. Figures 5–4, 5–5, 5–6, and 5–7 are examples of ads for specific businesses. Your sole objective in these ads is to get the telephone to ring. You want the ad to be broadly appealing, but, at the same time, you want it to eliminate totally unqualified responses. The sample ads are of varying length and persuasiveness to suggest the range of possibilities. Buyers are more often interested in the cash required for down payment and the owners' cash flow than they are in the total price and the sales volume.

Rare Opportunity

Printing Company

Only $20,000 down. Owner will finance remainder.

If you are a qualified printer, your work can pay off the balance.

Unique situation.

(Broker name)

Figure 5–4. Sample Advertisement

Restaurants and Other

Food Service Businesses

Over the last few weeks our brokers have been active listing and selling restaurants and other food service businesses. We have several other businesses for sale. They range from small roadside operations to large restaurants with real estate.

Our activity has also produced many well qualified buyers who are seeking special kinds of restaurants and food service situations.

If you are interested in buying *or* selling a restaurant, convenience store, delicatessen, or food market, please call us.

(Broker name)

Figure 5–5. Sample Advertisement

For Sale

Very Special

Womans' Fashion Store

Superb New Canaan location.

Volume $400,000 per year.

Owner asking $75,000 plus modest inventory. Owner will help you finance and will train you.

(Broker name)

Figure 5–6. Sample Advertisement

Advertisements that stress the benefits to the buyer—security, enjoyment, self-realization—rather than the features of the business—high profits, established customer list, good location—usually generate a better response. Unfortunately, time, space, and cost require ads to be succinct as well as effective, so choose your words carefully.

This concludes the discussion of finding buyers for specific businesses. In business sales you also need to find and build a pool of general buyers.

Landscape, Nursery, Florist

With 5-Bedroom Residence

Live in a colonial 5-bedroom home and walk down the path to direct the operations of your own business.

Here is a lifestyle packaged and ready for you on three acres of prime Northern Fairfield County real estate.

The property has been carefully landscaped by the present owner. It includes an appealing spring-fed pond that irrigates three greenhouses. There is ample additional land to display nursery stock and three frame buildings that will support expanding flower and greenhouse sales with office equipment and refrigerated display cases. The business already generates $100,000 in cash flow, but owner illness has prevented planned expansion, for which all the needed assets are in place.

The business is poised for growth in an expanding, high-income market. Your nursery will be easily spotted from the busy state highway.

This superb real estate, the large house, and the business opportunity can all be yours for $695,000, and the owner will finance up to half your purchase.

(Broker name)

Figure 5–7. Sample Advertisement

FINDING AND MANAGING A POOL OF GENERAL BUYERS

It bears repeating that many business buyers, unlike most real estate buyers, do not have a specific business purchase in mind, nor do they have any definite timetable for action. With patience (and good qualifying techniques), these general buyers can become real buyers for specific businesses. Three techniques are very effective in attracting the general buyer: networking, special events, and advertising.

NETWORKING

In addition to joining specific networks for specific business buyers (the restaurant example), you should consider more general business networks.

A very effective and relatively new network phenomenon is the "Tips Club." This is typically a group of 10 to 30 people who represent noncompeting businesses. Meetings are most often weekly early morning sessions over coffee, and they last about an hour. The club has only one purpose and that is to generate business for its members. Members are expected to patronize each other as much as is practical, but the real objective is for members to bring business leads and tips to each meeting. Members often ask for help with special leads and introductions. Some clubs have tough requirements for continued membership. Really effective clubs have a waiting list for membership. Forming a new club is a simple matter of getting a few business people together.

Other excellent groups are your Chamber of Commerce and similar civic-minded organizations. If your Board of Realtors has a commercial or investment division, it can be a good source of contacts for referrals. Business roundtable luncheons, university clubs, and professional societies are other groups that can produce a pool of general business buyers.

Merely joining a group does not automatically mean you will meet buyers or receive leads. In fact, except for "Tips" groups, joining a group just to receive a business advantage usually is not considered the proper motive for joining. Be sure you select groups that can benefit from your membership. Accept positions of responsibility when appropriate. To the best of your ability, put into the group at least as much as you get out of it.

Success in business networks depends on the same fundamentals as in real estate. You have to make sure people know what you do and that they have confidence in your abilities. Giving talks at meetings, distributing literature, and building individual relationships with other members are all good techniques. Find out how you can help other members achieve their objectives. *Your* objective requires that you build and maintain a list of people who are genuinely (if generally) interested in buying a business.

SPECIAL EVENTS

The subject of business ownership is interesting enough to attract people to seminars, lectures, and exhibits. In markets of almost any size, you can organize an event around this popular interest. As you did with the sellers' seminars, recruit others to participate. Team up with an accountant, an attorney, a banker, and an insurance agent who are also interested in developing more clients. Your team can develop a rather rich array of subjects to cover, subjects of real interest to anyone considering business ownership. You can publicize the seminar by word of mouth and by advertising. A title for such a seminar might be "Owning Your Own Business—How to Get Started."

While you may end up with some buyers for specific businesses you have listed, your objective should be to add to your pool of genuinely interested general buyers. Other special events might be done in conjunction with business opportunities shows or some business exhibits that are conducted in your area.

ADVERTISING

The majority of your pool of general buyers will come from the advertising you run. Advertising can create general awareness and name recognition, just as in real estate. The similarity with real estate extends to another aspect of advertising: Prospective buyers may call in response to a specific advertised listing but seldom will buy that listing. This well-recognized phenomenon produces substantial numbers of general buyers.

The General Buyer Ad

One very effective way to attract general buyers is to use a more general type of advertisement, as shown in Figure 5–8.

This advertising, like any other, needs to be run frequently and be well placed to do the best job. A weekly ad in the "Business Opportunities" section is typical. If you can afford a more elaborate advertising program—with display ads, billboards, or other media such as radio—establish a method to track the results and cost-effectiveness of your spending.

MANAGING YOUR POOL OF BUYERS

You probably already suspect that building a pool of buyers is a relatively easy task. Almost anyone would say yes to an offer of information about businesses for sale. The difficult part is qualifying these people in terms of their seriousness and capability as buyers and, as best you can, narrowing their focus of interest.

**Mind Your Own
Business**

If 1991 is the year you want to become independent and enjoy the freedom and rewards of owning your own business, we have dozens of BUSINESSES FOR SALE.

Distribution

Retail

Service

Wholesale

Restaurants

The businesses range in price from $15,000 to $6,000,000. Most will be financed by the seller.

Take the first step.

Call us.

(Broker Identification)

Businesses for Sale

All Types and Sizes

Most with Seller Financing

Call for Appointment

(Broker Identification)

Figure 5–8. The General Buyer Advertisement

One very effective qualifying screen may sound strange to people with real estate experience, but it is necessary to eliminate the very casual "tire kickers." The prospective buyer should expend some effort to get into your pool. You are about to devote a great deal of time and energy to help someone who may never be a customer. You need assurance that you are not wasting your time.

One simple way to get the prospective buyer to act is to require him or her to come to your office. Do not discuss the business buying process or any listings over the telephone. If the caller won't come to see you, you can assume he or she is not serious. In some large markets, there are so many people who are just curious about businesses that general telephone calls (and even specific advertisement response calls) require the salesperson to do a fairly thorough job of qualifying callers over the telephone.

Chapters 6 and 7 will present in detail the process of qualifying buyers. The general buyer may not be ready for full qualification at your first meeting, but you can inform him or her that you will need to know some facts in order to present the right kinds of businesses. A general idea of finances, a summary of experience, and an indication of how soon the person would act can give you enough of a feel to decide whether the person is serious and to narrow the focus of business size and type.

Your goal is to fully qualify everyone in your pool and to requalify them periodically. Asking people to update their information annually is one easy way to require effort. Those who do not provide an update, or who have not been in contact with you for, say, a year, can be removed from your pool.

THE RESULTS OF GOOD BUYER MANAGEMENT

Once you can maintain a well-qualified pool of buyers, you have the permanent foundation for your business. You can make periodic mailings to promote a variety of listings, and you can use the existence of your buyer pool when talking with potential sellers. It is most valuable, however, in turning prospective buyers into actual buyers. Every new listing you obtain can be promoted to the fully qualified buyers you have in your pool. Now you can reach your buyers quickly, easily, and inexpensively.

6

Working with Buyers

Business buyers share some traits with real estate buyers but are very different in others. Both are making major financial decisions and are very cautious. Neither business nor real estate buyers really know what they can afford nor the best way to finance their purchases. Both can sometimes appear capricious and irrational.

As for the differences, one important difference between them is their need for analysis of their purchase. Business buyers need much more financial analysis than do real estate buyers, and they need help doing it. Business buyers, even more than real estate buyers, don't really know what they want. Business buyers need to maintain confidentiality; real estate buyers do not. Probably the most significant single difference between the two kinds of buyers is this: Real estate buyers *need* to buy a house—business *buyers do not need* to buy a business. This chapter will show how these similarities and differences determine the way you must work with business buyers.

DUAL AGENCY

One important factor in business opportunities and real estate is the minimal amount of cobrokering. This means you will be working with both the buyer and seller in many instances. To repeat, this can present difficulties in maintaining your agency responsibility to your seller client.

The National Association of Realtors has prepared a booklet entitled *Who Is My Client?* It is a guide to compliance with the laws of agency. It covers definitions of agents, subagents and various agency relationships. It stresses the duties owed by an agent to his or her other principals; these are *loyalty, obedience, disclosure, confidentiality, reasonable care and diligence,* and *accounting.* It is especially important to remember that the agent must at *all times act solely* in the best interest of the principal to the exclusion of all other interests, including the agent's own interests. The buyer must understand that you represent the seller. In some cases you will in fact work for the buyer. The buyer will pay your commission and give you your instructions. A form for a buyer–finder agreement is shown as Appendix F. If you are the buyer's agent, you must tell the seller. Of course, you can also tell the seller that because you represent the buyer, the buyer will pay the commission.

AN OVERVIEW OF WORKING WITH BUYERS

You will perform many functions for the business buyer, even though you represent the seller. Here is a list:

- Educate
- Qualify—both personally and financially
- Help define criteria
- Help search for a business
- Help analyze the business
- Help find financing
- Help structure and negotiate the offer
- Manage the closing
- Provide after-purchase help

It should now be clear why care is urged in observing the laws of agency. It is easy to think of the buyers as your clients when you do so much work for them. Another reason you will get close to your buyers is because they will be with you over a long period of time. Earlier in this book, it was mentioned that business buyers do not have to buy any particular business. They can wait as long as necessary until they find exactly what they want. You will need to build long-term relationships with business buyers.

EDUCATING THE BUYER

Most real-estate buyers have a reasonably good idea of what real estate people do, how the market works, how price is determined, where to get money, and what services a real-estate brokerage firm offers. This is not the case with most business buyers. You will have to educate them on how the business buying process works and what functions you are prepared to perform.

QUALIFYING THE BUYER

This is the single most important step in dealing with business buyers. Not only do these buyers need to be qualified financially (see Chapter 7), they need to be qualified personally.

If they know (or think they know) what kind of business they want, find out if they have the knowledge, skills, and traits required to be successful at it. When they don't know what kind of business they want, help them define their criteria. The first steps involve understanding a buyer's knowledge, skills, and traits, and learning why business ownership is being considered in the first place.

Why do buyers want to own a business? Why do they think they can be successful? The specter of real or potential severance from employment is only one reason to consider owning a business. Owning a business can mean independence, the opportunity to excel, a chance to do what one wants, a way to build for one's self and one's family, and the satisfaction of setting and meeting one's own goals. It can also be the best investment one can make under the new tax laws. Of course, owning a business doesn't automatically mean wealth, happiness, and financial security.

Whether buyers see themselves standing among the plantings in their tree nursery, consulting with their staff in their electronics plant, winning a major client for their agency, or greeting guests in their restaurant, they should know that technology and competition can affect any business. Owning a business can mean long hours and high financial risk. Stress can affect the entrepreneur as much as the employee.

The major difference in owning a business is one of personal control. Instead of reacting to a situation with feelings of impotence, as is often the case for an employee, a business owner can take action and make choices and decisions. While the outcome may be no better, most competent, productive people, if given a choice, would bet on themselves to do the best job of looking out for their own interests. Concerns about health and stress, a desire to be more involved with family, and a strong need to set one's own personal standards of conduct and performance can all potentially be satisfied by owning a business.

Before you spend a lot of time with prospective buyers, you should take a moment to ask them why they want to own a business. They have at least six other alternatives: a different job, a different company, consulting, teaching, government service, or even retirement. Their reasons may vary from security to wealth. While there are no right or wrong reasons, it is important to know why someone wants his or her own business. Owning a business had better satisfy these basic criteria or that person will be no better off than he or she is now. Worksheet 3, at the end of the chapter, will help you focus your buyer's thoughts on these fundamental criteria.

Buyers want businesses that they can enjoy owning and managing. However, to be able to manage it at all, they need to have, or be willing to get, the essential knowledge and skills required to do so. Start by suggesting that your buyers take a personal inventory. Our sample inventory is purposely divided into three parts: knowledge, skills, and traits (use Worksheet 4 at the end of the chapter):

1. *Knowledge*: Don't let your buyer restrict this list to the work experience. Family, sports, hobbies, vacations, or other interests all provide knowledge. Ask him or her this question: "What five things do you *know* more about than almost anybody?" Then have them rank the five responses. While you're at it, go ahead and ask the buyer to list five things about which he or she knows the least. Most find this an easy list to develop.

2. *Skills:* The same ground rules apply. This time, the question for your buyers is: "What five things can you *do* better than almost

anybody?" Have your buyers do the reverse list of things they do poorly. It's a harder exercise than you might think, and it will be helpful later in recognizing skills as well as deficiencies.

3. *Traits:* The buyer should complete this sentence five times, "I am . . . " Tell them to concentrate on physical and mental attributes.

The separation of these three categories has been done to emphasize the differences among them. Knowledge can usually be acquired by study. If you want to see whether you have some particular knowledge, you can take a test or answer some questions. Skills, on the other hand are things that you do—arts, crafts, or special abilities—especially ones using the hands or body. Skills come from practice.

While most people can reasonably expect to acquire knowledge by studying, there is no such expectation that a person can acquire skills by practicing. For example: You can study and learn all there is to know about juggling, but you may never have the skills to do it well, no matter how much you practice. Although you may improve, you may still remain relatively unskilled.

This distinction becomes important when we are looking at the essential requirements of a business. If a buyer is deficient in some required knowledge (knowledge of all the sizes and styles in a product line of dresses), he or she can probably overcome it. If a buyer is deficient in a required skill (selling those dresses to buyers), it may be more cause for concern.

And what about traits? Traits are qualities that describe a person's makeup or personality, such as "honest, "people-oriented," "self-starter," and "highly motivated." There is little a person can do to change his or her traits, and only two seem essential to success:

1. *Physical.* Buyers *will* need to have whatever level of health and energy the business and their objectives require.

2. *Mental.* Most businesses don't require super intelligence, but buyers should be alert for special requirements, such as creativity in an advertising agency or fashion sense in a business involving style or design.

THE MYTH OF THE ENTREPRENEURIAL "TYPE"

Now a few words about comparing buyers with entrepreneurs. You've probably heard the stereotypical descriptions of entrepreneurs. Because the descriptions are so exaggerated, you would bet you could recognize one of these super humans on sight (most likely by the glint in the eye and the brash, self-assured walk). There are even tests that can compare people to the profile of a successful entrepreneur.* But the profiles turn out to exhibit a remarkable similarity to the profile of *any* successful business person, which shouldn't be surprising. Good work habits, tenacity, a solid sense of self, and reasonable risk-taking are always valuable traits, and little is ever accomplished without strong desire.

Like any successful group of business people, entrepreneurs have personality traits that range from shy to pugnacious, from workaholic to sloth, and from vivacious to dull as a stone. Some were previous failures, and some have been winners at everything they've tried. Some are driven by insecurity; others can't even imagine failure.

There are extreme definitions of *entrepreneur* that restrict the term to the creators of new enterprises. Other definitions are broad enough to include anyone who bears the ultimate risk of a business. It's important to put this idea of the successful entrepreneurial type into perspective. There are no easy checklists that can eliminate or excuse a person from considering business ownership or that can guarantee that someone has the "right stuff." Other than strong desire, there is no special common denominator.

WHAT IT ALL MEANS

After you have thoroughly reviewed your buyer's knowledge, skills, and traits, reflect on the analysis from Worksheet 4. Remember, there is no right way to look on paper. Successful entrepreneurs are as varied as any group of people. None of them probably has any more total knowledge or skills than your buyer; it's just that what he or she does have is very relevant to his or her business.

Here are two more reasons not to disqualify a buyer too quickly: First, one kind of knowledge or skill can sometimes be substituted

---

*Those who want to conduct a more in-depth personal assessment can obtain self-scoring profile questionnaires from:

The American Entrepreneurs Assoc.   or
2311 Pontius Avenue
Los Angeles, CA 90064

The Center for Entrepreneurial
    Management
83 Spring Street
New York, NY 10012

for another. For example, one buyer may not have great face to face selling skills but may possess exceptional skills at managing sales people. One buyer may not know all the markets for the product but may know how to manufacture it better than most people. The second reason not to get discouraged is that your buyer can usually hire people who do have the knowledge and skills he or she may lack (including the former owner). Hiring to get critical knowledge and skills is common, but there is one major risk for the owner. If the knowledge and skills are *really* critical, and if the owner is relying nearly 100 percent on someone else, he or she can become a hostage to that employee.

In summary, get a good feel for your buyer's knowledge and skills. Be prepared to rule out situations obviously outside a person's competence but keep the gates as wide open as possible in the early stages. This inventory of knowledge, skills, and traits is where you end up when you use the conventional elements to determine what kind of business a person should buy. Any business description based on these elements will directly reflect past experience and be very general, which is fine as a beginning. Whatever definition you have formed has properly eliminated some extremes and is based on a degree of logic.

SETTING THE REAL CRITERIA

There are some less conventional criteria that can truly trigger a positive or negative response to a business opportunity. These are the more specific things buyers think about when evaluating a business. Worksheet 5 at the end of this chapter will help with this important task. As personal as it might be, you must look at how much money your buyer wants to make. First, however, you should understand clearly the difference between how much money someone *needs* and how much money someone *wants*.

HOW MUCH MONEY YOUR BUYER NEEDS

The temptation here is to add up current expenses and use that figure to determine how much is needed. The fact is, one can always cut back. Cutting back can vary from eliminating some luxuries to completely redoing one's lifestyle. Have your buyers do a zero-based budget in which they examine everything from the private schools their children attend to how often they go to the movies. Only they can say whether or not something is essential. They may find it useful to prepare two budgets, one that they would like to have and one that represents an absolute minimum.

You should be aware that some business buyers have such a strong desire and commitment that they have sold everything and lived with just the barest essentials in order to keep their needs for money low. You and your buyer should also know that business ownership offers opportunities to shift certain insurance, automobile, legal, accounting, and other expenses to the business. If the business is successful, it can also provide employment and perks for family members.

Be as accurate as you can when you help your buyers decide how much money they need. It is a critical factor in the final decision to buy or not buy a business. If they overstate how much they need, they may miss a great opportunity. If they understate their needs, they could buy a business and end up in financial distress. Worksheet 5, Section A, will help your buyers determine how much money they *need* to earn.

It is important that both you and your buyers understand how the family fits into this entire process of buying a business. Your buyer's family may react with some surprise and anxiety when they are told what your buyer is considering. If your buyer is the principal wage earner, the family's concerns will be heightened.

Anyone buying a business needs to explain his or her great desire to the family. A family's objections often then become touched with guilt. Buyers need to encourage their families to open up about their concerns. It's best if they can be involved in the decision. You may want to advise your buyers to have their families participate in completing the various worksheets suggested. Buyers should share with their families their expectations about how the family and its lifestyle are going to be affected; should talk with their families about money, family time, and the stresses expected; and should share their vision of the opportunity and what it could mean to them and their families. Above all, your buyers should explain the risks. To gain family support and help, your buyer must ask for it, particularly if this is the first time the family has been involved in your buyer's business dealings. He or she should pay attention to the family's concerns, and family members should pay attention to how much your buyer wants to do this.

HOW MUCH MONEY YOUR BUYER WANTS

This single factor can be the most definitive screening criteria. For example, if your buyer wants a business that earns an annual minimum of $500,000 today, you have eliminated all but a few individual retail businesses and nearly any business that could be bought for less than $2 million.

How much money your buyer wants to earn has the added dimension of time and can't be totally separated from other criteria. Here are four examples to demonstrate:

1. Your buyer wants a company that will provide a nice living, year after year. If the business does well, the buyer will probably trade off any higher earnings for working less.

2. Your buyer wants a company with a present cash flow adequate to cover his or her needs, but it has to be able to grow. Your buyer's targets are $100,000 in three years and $200,000 in five years. After that, who knows?

3. Your buyer doesn't care if the business is losing money right now. The objective is a business that can grow into a multi-million dollar enterprise. Without that potential, your buyer isn't going to give up his or her present situation.

4. It really depends on what your buyer is doing. If he or she can find a business in the perfect locations, one involved in a favorite area of interest, or one that satisfies some criteria for status, travel, or the like, the money is relatively unimportant.

In fact, your buyer will probably be somewhere in between these examples. What's important right now is to convert your buyer's income desires into criteria against which you can measure the businesses you are going to consider. Worksheet 5, Section B, will help your buyers determine what they want to earn. Now that you and your buyer have set criteria to cover how much money your buyer needs and wants, start on the other criteria.

LOCATION

This simplest of criterion needs to be considered in two ways to determine whether the location suits your buyer *(search criterion)* and whether it suits the business *(evaluation criterion)*.

Search criterion. The three general models are:

1. Your buyer wants businesses only within a commute of his or her present home.

2. Your buyer is willing to relocate anywhere (or somewhere) for the right business.

3. Your buyer wants to relocate to some specific area.

Buyers are tempted to look at every good opportunity, no matter where it is. You might ask, "What is the harm in that?" The harm is that it takes time and effort from you, the buyer, the seller, and advisors. Good contacts, for example, will be less inclined to bring opportunities to you if they feel you and your buyers waste their time by looking at businesses you will never really pursue.

Evaluation Criterion

You and your buyer should be concerned about whether the location is a plus or minus for the specific business you are considering. Each business will have different needs for street visibility, traffic, parking, ease of access, neighborhood surroundings, proximity of competition, and labor availability. Mention should be made here about the risk of moving a newly purchased business. It is a potentially costly proposition. The new owner may lose key employees, customers, vendors, and community relationships. The new buyer of a business has plenty to contend with already. Some businesses *can* be moved and others *should* be moved, but most should be left where they are, at least until the buyer is established in the business. Use Worksheet 5, Section C to evaluate location.

RISK

The most complex of the criteria to establish, *risk* has many dimensions, one of which needs special explanation. This dimension of risk is called *risk preference*. The easiest way to understand it is through an analogy with flipping a coin. The odds are 50/50 each time a coin is flipped no matter how much is bet. A person who is comfortable betting a dollar or two might never consider betting a thousand dollars, even though the odds are still the same and the money might still double. Some people prefer to invest very little in high-risk/high-return ventures; others prefer this type. Any investment has the phenomenon of risk attached to it, and unless you are aware of this idea of risk preference, you might not be able to understand your buyer's criteria of risk.

The better-known dimensions of risk are the risk of losing an investment and the risk of not earning a *return* on an investment. (Return is not only the earnings on the investment but the appreciation in value of the investment as well.) Buying a business with a lot of readily saleable assets (a machine shop with standard equipment or a liquor store with normal inventory) provides a lower risk *of* investment than does purchasing an advertising agency or a real-estate firm, both of which have few assets. However, the machine shop and the liquor store are rather fixed in the ways they can earn a return *on* investment and therefore are more risky in this dimension than the advertising agency and real-estate firm, which have wider ranges of earning behavior and less fixed expense to carry. There is one last thing to consider when thinking about risk. If your buyer plans to manage the business, he or she is also risking *time*.

Remember, you are not calculating rates of return or computing your buyer's probability of success in a specific business yet; you are establishing criteria regarding risk. Even assuming that you and your buyer's advisors will structure the purchase to limit risks as much as possible, you must prepare your buyer to take some degree of risk. In summary, then, your buyer has *assets* and *time* to invest for a *return*. There is no mathematical formula to set this criteria, but you should develop qualitative descriptions of the degree of risk your buyer is prepared to take. Use Worksheet 5, Section D to analyze your buyer's risk preference.

LIQUIDITY

Unlike risk, *liquidity* is a straightforward issue; that is, how quickly could the business be converted to cash? No business provides the liquidity of stocks, bonds, or other similar investments, but some businesses have more liquidity than others. A distribution business with stock being held on consignment can be converted to cash easily; a rental apartment complex may take many months.

Once again, you are not yet evaluating businesses, just establishing criteria for liquidity. You should determine if your buyer is liable to face any sudden obligations or investment opportunities requiring cash. If your buyer doesn't provide for cash needs, he or she could be forced to sell assets or the entire company under "fire-sale" conditions. Use Worksheet 5, Section E to help your buyer examine the issue of liquidity.

GROWTH POTENTIAL

A business's potential for growth is a very useful criterion because it is a very good screen. If your buyer requires a "sky's-the-limit" business, you are not going to show an historic bed-and-breakfast inn on the seacoast of Maine. This is not to say that a business that is small today can't be expanded. That's the very essence of potential. Many businesses can be expanded physically, geographically, and conceptually. In fact, almost any business can grow to some extent. However, the practical facts are that some businesses lend themselves to growth through easy replication, fast-growing markets, or competitive advantage, while others do not. Your task is to decide what your buyer needs for growth potential in the business you are going to seek. Use Worksheet 5, Section F for this exercise.

PHYSICAL AND OTHER WORKING CONDITIONS

Most people can be somewhat flexible in the area of physical and other working conditions, but make sure you know your buyer's limits. A screw machine shop can require 12-hour days in the factory, a wine distributorship can mean five days a week on the road, and owning a company that consults on fundraising could easily lead to several nights a week attending meetings.

To some buyers, working predictable hours that allow for family or hobbies is an important criterion. Some buyers feel they are at a stage where comfortable surroundings do matter. On the other hand, some may be willing to work nights and weekends from a briefcase in the corner of a warehouse. One aspect of working conditions can be quantified. You can calculate what a luxurious office suite, plush furniture, and a private secretary cost. In metropolitan centers, the costs could exceed $40,000 per year:

Rent on 800 square feet at $20 per foot	$16,000
Private secretary	25,000
$10,000 in furnishings (5-year life)	2,000
Total	$43,000

No matter where your buyer is on the scale, the physical environment and working conditions of a company are important components of your buyer's future satisfaction. Use Worksheet 5, Section G to examine this criterion.

STATUS AND IMAGE

The status and image derived from owning a particular business varies from person to person. When buying a business, a buyer should be excited about seeing himself or herself as the owner. Some people would rather own a break-even newspaper than a very profitable, high-volume gas station/convenience store. For others, the business will have to be large; still others want something glamorous. There are no rights or wrongs in this arena. Just be sure you honestly match the business to your buyer's needs for status and image. Use Worksheet 5, Section H to help your buyer analyze his or her needs for status and image.

PEOPLE INTENSITY

"The more people, the more problems," say many business owners. People problems can result from the difficulty in managing a large work force. Ask the owner of a large real-estate company or the night shift manager of an industrial cleaning service. People problems can also result from a lack of workers to fill job openings. In Fairfield County, Connecticut, for example, workers for fast-food stores, supermarkets, and shopping centers are being bussed in from surrounding counties. A lack of affordable housing in the county may perpetuate this situation for some time. If a business is dependent on the number and quality of the people that can be attracted and retained as employees, your buyer needs to be comfortable managing people. To some buyers, this is an important criterion of the business. Worksheet 5, Section I will focus your buyer on this criterion.

COMPETITIVE ENVIRONMENT

No business is completely without competition, but there are extremes. At one end are businesses in large markets that face competition everywhere. Food service is an example. In any market there are restaurants, fast-food franchises, delicatessens, and even supermarkets, all competing for the same customers. At the other extreme are special niche businesses in relatively small markets. A company that makes turntables for revolving restaurants is an example of this kind of business. If the extent of competition is important to your buyer, make it a part of the search criteria. Use Worksheet 5, Section J to assess your buyer's feelings about competition.

SPECIFIC BUSINESS CONTENT

Your buyer may have special requirements for the business. Perhaps it has to be involved in a specific field so that your buyer can capitalize on his or her experience. Maybe it has to serve some social goal. Your buyer may want a manufacturing business or may want to exclude restaurants. He or she might want to be involved in or avoid high technology, international dealings, or some other special element of business. The point is, if something is important, make it a part of the business criteria.

The content of the business, what it is and what it does, is really at the heart of determining what kind of business your buyer wants. Spend a lot of time on it. It's going to be the main starting point in your search for a business. Encourage your buyer to dream. This is the time to consider what your buyer really wants to do with his or her life. Go beyond the obvious. An executive who loves to cook might make a lousy restaurateur but could publish a great newsletter on kitchen appliances and utensils. A pet fancier might never be able to become a veterinarian but could own a boarding kennel or grooming salon, or a chain of them. If the outdoor life is for your buyer, he or she doesn't have to become a Forest Ranger. There are tree service companies; fishing lodges; lawn, landscaping, and yard care firms; fencing companies; and many others. While owning businesses in fields they love is no guarantee that your buyers will be good at them, the added enthusiasm that comes from doing something they thoroughly enjoy can help them succeed.

Don't let your buyer become too rigid. You may initially determine that your buyer wants a manufacturing company, but remember, this is only one of several criteria. At this stage, you probably aren't aware of the many kinds of businesses that exist that might really make your buyer happy. If you have never worked with the Standard

Industrial Classification (SIC) system, you should review the descriptions in this most widely used method of classifying businesses. You'll find it at your local library. Just reviewing the names of these business types can spark ideas for you and your buyer. Your local Yellow Pages are another source of ideas.

Encourage your buyer to be patient. If someone wants to own a large commercial printing firm, that person might start off by owning a small quick-print shop. A buyer who wants to eventually own a telecommunications company could get started by buying a small interconnect business or an answering service. The important thing is to get into the proper arena. Then your buyer can get familiar with the market, the suppliers, the competitors, and the customers. This is how a person finds the next opportunity, and builds the base to take advantage of it. Use Worksheet 5, Section K to establish these criteria.

WORKSHEET 3

Why Do You Want to Own Your Own Business?

For each of the following statements, mark your degree of agreement; 0 equals no agreement at all and 5 equals complete agreement.

Statement of Reason	Degree of Agreement 0–5
I just can't stand to work for anyone anymore.	_____
I'm tired/bored doing what I'm doing.	_____
I want to get (very) rich.	_____
I feel insecure working for someone else.	_____
I want something I can really commit to.	_____
I have good reason to know that I can handle risk, especially personal risk.	_____
I don't like being around so many people.	_____
I want to work less (more).	_____
I want to travel less (more).	_____
I want to build something of my own.	_____
I can afford to fail.	_____
I would like the feeling of owning my own business.	_____
I want to move somewhere else.	_____
I can do without status symbols.	_____
I have an idea/a concept I want to pursue.	_____
I want to do something that can really grow.	_____
I want to stand out.	_____
I feel like a servant.	_____
I want to be properly rewarded for my efforts.	_____
I want to build something my family can get involved in.	_____
I don't like the politics and inefficiencies of corporate life.	_____
I want a lifestyle with more _____ and less _____	_____
I have full family support in this effort.	_____
I don't like being so dependent on others.	_____
I've tried finding a job and can't find what I want.	_____
I'll never get promoted where I am.	_____
I'd gladly pinch pennies if I had to.	_____
I don't like all the organizational competition.	_____
I'm being held back working for someone else.	_____
Other: _____	

The purpose of this worksheet is to help you articulate your feelings and to start you thinking about the benefits and drawbacks of having your own business. Scoring your answers is simply a way to see which of them is important to you. When you are done, complete these sentences:

I want my own business because _____

_____

_____

I think I can be successful in my own business because _____

_____

_____

There are two ways the worksheet can be used:

1. Use this analysis to think through whether owning a business will satisfy the reasons you gave for considering it. For example, if you don't like being dependent on others, owning your own business is no guarantee you'll be free of dependency. You may become very dependent on customers or key employees. Owning a business entails much risk. You may want to consider just changing jobs.

2. Save this analysis to check against specific companies you will uncover later. After all your search and work, if the company can't satisfy these basic emotional criteria, you might want to reconsider.

Reprinted from *How to Leave Your Job and Buy A Business of Your Own* by C. D. Peterson, published by the McGraw-Hill Book Company. Copyright © 1988 McGraw-Hill, Inc. Reprinted with permission.

Personal Inventory

A. KNOWLEDGE—THINGS YOU KNOW

What five things do you know more about than almost anybody?

1. _____
2. _____
3. _____
4. _____
5. _____

And less about?

1. _____
2. _____
3. _____
4. _____
5. _____

B. SKILLS—THINGS YOU CAN DO

What five things can you do better than almost anybody?

1. _____
2. _____
3. _____
4. _____
5. _____

And less well?

1. _____
2. _____
3. _____
4. _____
5. _____

C. TRAITS—THINGS YOU ARE

I am

1. _____
2. _____
3. _____
4. _____
5. _____

I am not

1. _____
2. _____
3. _____
4. _____
5. _____

D. WHAT THE INVENTORY MEANS

The inventory suggests I should consider these kinds of business situations:

1. _____
2. _____
3. _____

And avoid these:

1. _____
2. _____
3. _____

(Note: If your spouse or another family member will be part of this effort at business ownership, repeat the form for him or her.)

Reprinted from *How to Leave Your Job and Buy A Business of Your Own* by C. D. Peterson, published by the McGraw-Hill Book Company. Copyright © 1988 McGraw-Hill, Inc. Reprinted with permission.

WORKSHEET 5

Setting Your Criteria

Complete the top portion of each criterion in Worksheet 6 now and save it. Complete the bottom portion, rating your candidate company, once you find one, from 1 to 10 (10 is best).

A. HOW MUCH MONEY YOU NEED

	Minimum Amount	Desired Amount
Housing (primary home)	$_____	$_____
Utilities	_____	_____
Transportation	_____	_____
Food (in home)	_____	_____
Meals (outside of home)	_____	_____
Clothing	_____	_____
Education	_____	_____
Entertainment/vacations	_____	_____
Medical & hygiene expenses (est.)	_____	_____
Life insurance	_____	_____
Health insurance	_____	_____
Other insurance	_____	_____
Dues, memberships, donations	_____	_____
Maintenance, cleaning, laundry	_____	_____
Debt repayments	_____	_____
Savings	_____	_____
Other	_____	_____
Other	_____	_____
Total	$_____	$_____

Company ratings:

Your candidate company has an estimated cash flow available to an owner of $_____

Your candidate company rates _____
         (1 to 10)

(Note: Be sure you are comparing your needs and the candidate's cash flow on the same tax basis.)

B. HOW MUCH MONEY YOU WANT

Consider amount, growth, and risk.

Year 1 $_____   Year 3 $_____   Year 5 $_____
Year 2 $_____   Year 4 $_____

Company rating:

You estimate that your candidate company can provide:

Year 1 $_____   Year 3 $_____   Year 5 $_____
Year 2 $_____   Year 4 $_____

Your candidate company rates _____
         (1 to 10)

C. LOCATION

Search criterion:
1. Must be within _____ miles.
2. Can be in _____ or _____
3. Can be anywhere; I will move.
4. I am prepared to relocate the business if I have to.
   Evaluation c riterion: Consider visibility, traffic, parking, ease of access, neighborhood surroundings, proximity of competition, and labor availability.

Company Rating:
Your candidate company location is _____
Your candidate company rates _____
$$(1 \text{ to } 10)$$

D. RISK PREFERENCE

For an acceptable opportunity:

I am prepared to risk $_____ in total, with $_____ down payment and _____ years of work.

For an excellent opportunity:

I am prepared to risk $_____ in total, with $_____ down payment and _____ years of work.

Assuming a typical business opportunity with a normal degree of risk, I can mark myself on this scale (1–10):

| |____ |____ |____ |____ |____ |____ |____ |____ |____ |____
1   2   3   4   5   6   7   8   9   10

I will risk some of my savings   I will risk it all
but not my house or other   to have my own
possessions.   business.

Company Rating:

Your candidate company requires $_____ in total, with $_____ down payment and a potential commitment of _____ years.
Your candidate company rates _____
$$(1 \text{ to } 10)$$

E. LIQUIDITY

Annual Personal and Family Cash Requirements

Year	Known*	Probable	Possible
1	$_____	$_____	$_____
2	_____	_____	_____
3	_____	_____	_____
4	_____	_____	_____
5	_____	_____	_____

*This amount can come from Worksheet 6A, "How much money you need." If you face sudden requirements for cash, your business needs to be easily able to be converted to cash or to be sold.

Company Rating:

Year	Estimated Cash Flow from Normal Operations	Estimated Additional Cash Available through Liquidation of Assets	Total
Historical average	$_____	NA	$_____
1	_____	$_____	_____
2	_____	_____	_____
3	_____	_____	_____
4	_____	_____	_____
5	_____	_____	_____

Your candidate company rates _____
(1 to 10)

F.   GROWTH POTENTIAL

My basic objective is to live well. If (when) the business has sales of $_____ and an owner's cash flow of $_____, all I will want is enough growth to keep the business healthy.

I eventually want a business with sales of approximately $_____ and an owner's cash flow of about $_____. The business I buy needs to be capable of reaching that level in _____ years.

My objective is to build a very large company very quickly. Any business I buy must have at least $_____ in sales and $_____ in owner's cash flow now and in five years should have $_____ in sales and $_____ in owner's cash flow.

Company Rating:
Your candidate company is estimated to have this growth potential:

Year	Sales	Owner's Cash Flow
Present Level	$_____	$_____
1	_____	_____
2	_____	_____
3	_____	_____
4	_____	_____
5	_____	_____

Your candidate company rates _____
(1 to 10)

G.   PHYSICAL WORKING CONDITIONS:

The hours per week I want to work _____
The number of days per month I want to travel _____
The type of office or surroundings I want can best be described as _____
It is _____ is not _____ important that I avoid certain hazardous or physical conditions (check one).

Company Rating:
Your candidate company has these characteristics:
    Working hours per week _____

Days travel per month _____
Office/surroundings that can be described as _____
Hazardous or dangerous conditions that include _____
Your candidate company rates _____
(1 to 10)

H. STATUS AND IMAGE

	No	Doesn't Matter	Yes
I want:			
A business that will give me high visibility.	___	___	___
A business that is considered large or substantial.	___	___	___
A business that is more knowledge based (white collar) than skill based (blue collar).	___	___	___
A business involved in a sophisticated or glamorous field.	___	___	___
A business on the cutting edge of innovation.	___	___	___
A business that provides a service to the community and its people.	___	___	___

Company Rating:

Your candidate company:	Yes	No
Will give high visibility	___	___
Is considered large or substantial	___	___
Is a "white-collar" business	___	___
Is sophisticated/glamorous	___	___
Is on the cutting edge of innovation	___	___
Provides community or other service	___	___

Your candidate company rates _____
(1 to 10)

I. PEOPLE INTENSITY:

People Issue	My Degree of Comfort	
	Low	High
Recruiting, interviewing, hiring, training	___	___
Specialized skills supervision	___	___
Wage and salary administration	___	___
Union (labor) relations	___	___
Personnel policy development and administration	___	___
"Motivation," discipline, firing	___	___
Organization design and development	___	___
Conflict resolution, counseling	___	___
Recognition and incentives	___	___
High turnover, morale problems	___	___
OSHA, ERISA, etc.	___	___

Company Rating:

Your candidate company: Required Degree
People Issue   of Intensity

	Low	High
Recruiting, interviewing, hiring, training	____	____
Specialized skills supervision	____	____
Wage and salary administration	____	____
Union (labor) relations	____	____
Personnel policy development and administration	____	____
"Motivation," discipline, firing	____	____
Organization design and development	____	____
Conflict resolution, counseling	____	____
Recognition and incentives	____	____
High turnover, morale problems	____	____
OSHA, ERISA, etc.	____	____

Your candidate company rates _____
                               (1 to 10)

J.   COMPETITIVE ENVIRONMENT   Yes   No

	Yes	No
It is important that the business I buy is the only business (or one of the only businesses) of its type in the market area.	____	____
The business I buy must be the market share leader or near leader in its field.	____	____
I want a business with high barriers to entry for potential competitors.	____	____
I especially want protections such as patents and licenses.	____	____
The business should not be subject to inordinate foreign competition.	____	____
The business must measure up to competitors in terms or margins, productivity, modern equipment, etc.	____	____

Company Rating:

Your candidate company:

Has _____ competitors in its market.

Has _____ percent market share and ranks no. _____

Is in a field with high _____ low _____ barriers to entry.

Has patents or licenses: yes _____ no _____

Is subject to inordinate foreign competition: yes _____ no _____

Has competitive margins, productivity, equipment, etc.: yes _____ no _____

Your candidate company ranks _____
                          (1 to 10)

K.   SPECIFIC BUSINESS CONTENT:

The three things I have most enjoyed doing:

In my business career:

1. _____
2. _____
3. _____

As family or recreational activities:

1. _____
2. _____
3. _____

In academic pursuits:

1. _____
2. _____
3. _____

In community or public service:

1. _____
2. _____
3. _____

As fantasies:

1. _____
2. _____
3. _____

Based on these most-enjoyed activities and on my knowledge, skills, and traits, here are some kinds of businesses that either make, service, sell, consult, or are in some way a possible fit for me:

_____
_____
_____
_____
_____
_____
_____
_____
_____
_____

My "perfect company" would be:

_____
_____
_____
_____

Company rating:
What your candidate company does:

_____
_____
_____
_____

What it could do:

_____

_____

_____

_____

Your candidate company rates _____
                                (1 to 10)

(Note: If your spouse or another family member will be a part of this effort at business ownership, repeat form for him or her.)

CHAPTER 7

Qualifying the Buyer Financially

Your work with business buyers will require you not only to determine their present resources but to help them locate additional sources of money.

HOW MUCH MONEY THE BUYER HAS

Worksheet 6 can help you organize all the possible sources of money. The place to begin is with the wealth buyers may be surprised to know they already have:

1. **Cash** and the **near cash** available from publicly traded stocks and bonds are the easiest to calculate.

2. **Investments** of other types, such as rental real estate, represent another source of money.

3. **Assignable assets**, such as notes due or a time-sharing contract, can be converted to cash.

4. **Partnership interests** may allow for the buyer to cash in or sell out.

5. **Personal property** may represent considerable value that the buyer can convert to cash. Some determined people have sold almost everything they own in order to buy or start a business.

6. A **second job** is another source of cash used by determined people. Overtime, freelancing, and moonlighting might provide substantial cash in some cases.

7. A **working spouse**, in addition to contributing money, may also be able to provide medical and insurance coverage.

8. **Insurance policies** can be a surprising source of cash, particularly if they are older policies. Often they can be liquidated and replaced with new insurance products while giving cash to invest.

9. **Retirement accounts**—whether they are company managed, individual IRA and Keogh, or any other type—may have rules that allow the buyer to convert them into cash. Penalties may be involved, but the buyer should at least be aware of the potential availability.

10. **Income from trusts and annuities** is an obvious source of cash, but less obvious is the fact that this stream of income may be able to be capitalized and sold, thus giving the buyer a lump sum of cash to invest.

11. The **equity** in their homes is the significant cash yielding asset for most people. Rapid inflation in home values and the eagerness of financial institutions to lend against home equity have made cash readily available to the home owner in the form of equity credit lines, a refinanced first mortgage, or a second mortgage.

12. **Savings** are the final source of money buyers already have. Cutting back on club memberships, entertaining, and other luxuries is a first step, but if buyers are really committed to raising cash, they should consider a complete re-evaluation of their lifestyle.

Once you have added up all the money the buyer already has, it's time to see where he or she can borrow more.

WHERE TO BORROW PERSONALLY

First, consider opportunities for the buyer to borrow money personally:

1. **Friends** and **family** represent a common (if sometimes contentious) source of money. In addition to lending money, friends and family can provide financial support by guaranteeing borrowings from some other source. Cosigning an auto loan is an example familiar to most of us. In business transactions, the cosigner may have to pledge some specific asset, such as the equity in a house. Because the buyer is, in effect, "renting" someone else's wealth to be pledged, he or she should be prepared to pay for this financial support.

2. A **bank** or **credit union** may extend a personal line of credit.

3. A **margin/borrowing account** with a stock brokerage firm can be a borrowing source.

4. **Insurance policies** may have cash value that can be borrowed.

5. The **credit card** is a new source of borrowing. Some people receive dozens of unsolicited, pre-approved credit-card applications. With credit limits ranging from $1,000 to $5,000, this can represent significant credit. One Hollywood producer claims he produced his award winning film with the help of credit he had amassed from credit cards.

BORROWING THROUGH THE BUSINESS

While there are relatively few sources for personal borrowing, there are a tremendous number for businesses (the Resource Literature section at the back of the book offers extensive sources to locate both investors and lenders):

1. **Banks** are the most visible source of money. They lend money directly and indirectly through various guarantee programs. Banks can easily provide you with a description of their loan types and tell you their criteria.

2. **Asset lenders** and **factors** provide money against specific assets of the business. They may take a mortgage or lien on the asset, buy it outright at a discount (accounts receivable), or buy it and lease it back to the company.

3. The **Small Business Administration** (SBA) is an institution that should be understood by everyone in or considering a small business. It provides loans, loan guarantees, participation loans, and financial assistance. It assists state and local government programs to aid small businesses. It offers special programs to aid minorities. It also provides consulting services, training, government contract assistance, and a library of publications—all for little or no cost.

4. Other **federal agencies**, such as the Veterans Administration, the Department of Housing and Urban Development, and the U.S. Department of Agriculture offer a variety of programs.

5. Many **states** and some **cities** also offer loans, guarantees, and other assistance to small business. The departments responsible for these programs usually come under the heading of "economic development," "small business development," or "commerce." Some states and cities offer special grants or tax considerations to companies that participate in programs to create jobs, provide training, or assist minorities.

6. **Partners** are another source of money. Any decision on partnerships should be carefully reviewed by your buyer's advisors.

7. The **franchisor** is a potential lender if your buyer is considering a franchise.

8. A company's **suppliers**, if they sell on credit, are already lenders in a way. Extending the payment terms can generate money. Some suppliers can offer leases in place of sales as a way to reduce large cash requirements. Regular suppliers may be able to provide inventory on a consignment basis in which the business is invoiced only when it replaces sold stock.

9. Even **customers** can be sources of money. They can place orders early that might serve as collateral. They can lend money and accept repayment in goods and services.

10. The **landlord** might be a source of money. Deferring or forgiving some rent may be agreeable if the landlord's alternative is empty space. You and your buyer may be able to renegotiate the lease

to provide for lower rent now during the critical period but higher rent later when the business can better afford it. A variation on that idea is a lease tied to some percentage of sales. The base rent is lower than it would otherwise be, but if the business is successful, the landlord can receive much more than the regular market rent rate. This is common in a shopping center tenant lease.

11. **Insurance companies, foundations** and **the use of barter** are less common sources of money, but they may be available if the buyer's intended business has the characteristics to utilize them.

12. **Venture capitalists** are major sources of money. They lend and invest in companies that have a relatively high degree of risk so they can earn a higher-than-average rate of return. Their return may be in the form of interest, stock ownership, or consulting fees, but for many venture capital firms, the objective is to take the venture public. Sources of venture capital firms are contained in the Resources Literature section at the back of this book. Most of them have a published statement of their objectives and investment criteria. In addition, there are **venture groups** around the country that exist to bring investors together with investment opportunities. Some of these groups sponsor monthly luncheons where an open microphone is used to help those seeking funds and the investors to find each other.

13. **The seller** is the most common source of money for buying a business. Estimates are that 75 to 80 percent of all businesses sold are seller financed, and the percentage financed is between one-half and two-thirds of the selling price. Borrowing from the seller is easier, cheaper, and can often be for a longer term than with other sources. Sellers are willing to finance the sale partly because they understand and trust the collateral for the loan, which is the business being sold. Another reason for their willingness is the fact that right now *all* their investment is tied up in the business. Your buyer's purchase down payment will be some cash in hand. But the major reason sellers provide financing is to help sell the business and to sell it for more than they would get in an all-cash transaction. Sellers know that there are more potential buyers who can successfully operate the business and pay off a loan than there are potential buyers with resources to pay all cash.

HOW TO PERSUADE LENDERS OR INVESTORS

An axiom in negotiating and selling is "Find out what the other party wants." Common sense says that you are more likely to get what you want if the other party gets what he or she wants. You are also more able to develop alternatives the more fully you understand someone's true desires. Figure 7–1 will give you an idea of what typical lenders and investors want in terms of security.

Lenders and investors want to earn a *return on their investment*.

Source	With collateral inside business (accounts receivable, machinery, inventory, real estate, etc.)	With collateral outside business (home equity, stocks, insurance policies, etc.)	Unsecured (no collateral)	Percentage of equity (ownership in the new company)
Friends and family	x	x	x	x
Bank	x	x		
Margin or borrowing account		x		
Insurance policies		x		
Credit cards			x	
Asset lenders/factors	x			
SBA	x	x		
Federal agencies	x	x		
State and city agencies	x	x		
Partners				x
Employees			x	x
Suppliers	x		x	
Customers	x		x	
Landlord			x	
Insurance companies/foundations	x	x		
Venture capitalists	x	x		
The seller	x	x	x	x

Figure 7–1. Financing Matrix

Investors may be satisfied with little or no immediate return because their objective is long-term gain. Lenders usually want an immediate schedule of returns that will cover their cost of money and the risk premium of your loan.

Both lenders' and investors' objectives vary here on the subject of *repayment of principal (investment)*. Some will want scheduled repayment much like a mortgage; others will leave their money in the company indefinitely, content with the return they are (or will) receive, similar to a credit-card lender.

Security can be specific, such as a piece of machinery or the accounts receivable, or it can be general, such as a corporate or personal guarantee. Large, long-established businesses can borrow on a general line of credit, whereas smaller and less credit worthy companies are required to provide more specific security. *It's this fact that severely limits a buyer's ability to borrow money from a bank to finance the purchase of a small company that has few real assets to secure the loan.*

In terms of *equity participation*, most lenders don't want stock in the companies they finance. They are in the business of lending money. Investors, by definition, do own stock and are motivated to provide money, whether debt or equity, to increase the total value of their investment.

Your task is to learn from the financial sources what they want for return, repayment, security, and equity position and to select those that match your buyer's objectives and capabilities. Once you know what the sources want, you can help your buyer develop the presentation to address the issues of ability to repay and the provision of security.

THE APPLICATION PRESENTATION

The application for financing may be an informal meeting with the seller or a full business plan presentation to a venture capital firm. In either case your buyer needs to cover what he or she plans to do with the business and why he or she is qualified to do it. (The Resources Literature section at the back of the book gives you references to books and publications that can guide you through the development of a business plan.)

THE BUSINESS PLAN

A basic business plan outline might look like this:

1. A summary of the present situation
   The market(s)
   Competition
   The economy
   Current financial performance

2. An analysis of company strengths and weaknesses
   Management/people
   Products and services
   Facilities and equipment
   Financial resources
   Market position
   Technology
   Other departments and issues as appropriate

3. A description of what needs to be done
   Opportunities
   Threats
   Barriers
   Resources

4. A plan of action
   What will be done
   When
   By whom

5. Financial projections
   Income and expenses
   Balance sheet
   Source and application of cash

6. Measurements
   How will you measure results
   When
   What are the criteria of success

PERSONAL QUALIFICATIONS TO SUCCEED

Your buyer should submit a resume of his or her education, knowledge, skills, and experience, pointing out where the abilities match the needs of the business plan. Have the buyer also prepare a list of references that will be meaningful, listing people who can comment favorably on the buyer's business judgment, work habits, and reputation. If possible, the list should include people known to the lenders or investors.

One element that is essential to earning financiers' confidence is commitment. The buyer will need to submit a personal financial statement that shows both financial status and how much of it is being directed to the venture. Lenders and investors want to see that buyers believe strongly enough in themselves and their venture to fully commit to it.

The ultimate test of what a buyer is qualified to afford is a test for reasonableness that the Institute of Business Appraisers, in its publication *MO-9*, calls the Justification of Purchase Test. After investing the money one has and what one has borrowed, the business should generate enough cash to cover its operations, service the debt incurred, provide a return on the down payment, and afford a fair salary for the buyer's time. The answer is, of course, dependent on the specific company being considered and on the terms negotiated.

WORKSHEET 6

Sources of Money

A. MONEY YOU HAVE

	On Hand	Available
Cash, stocks, bonds	$_____	$_____
Other investments	_____	_____
Assignable assets	_____	_____
Partnership interests	_____	_____
Personal property	_____	_____
Second job income (annualized)	_____	_____
Spouse income	_____	_____
Insurance policies	_____	_____
Deferred compensation	_____	_____
Retirement accounts	_____	_____
Trusts and annuities	_____	_____
Equity in your home	_____	_____
What you can save (annualized)	_____	_____
TOTAL	_____	_____

B. WHERE YOU CAN BORROW

	Specific Contact	Potential Funds Available
Friends and family	_____	$_____
	_____	_____
Banks or credit union	_____	_____
	_____	_____
	_____	_____
Margin/borrowing account	_____	_____
	_____	_____
Insurance policies	_____	_____
	_____	_____
	_____	_____
Credit cards	_____	_____
	_____	_____
	_____	_____
Asset lenders and factors	_____	_____
	_____	_____
SBA	_____	_____
	_____	_____
	_____	_____

Other federal agencies   _____   _____

_____   _____

State and local agencies   _____   _____

_____   _____

Partners   _____   _____

_____   _____

Suppliers   _____   _____

_____   _____

Customers   _____   _____

_____   _____

Landlord   _____   _____

Insurance companies/foundations   _____   _____

_____   _____

Barter opportunities   _____   _____

_____   _____

Venture capitalists   _____   _____

_____   _____

Venture groups   _____   _____

_____   _____

The seller   _____   _____

     TOTAL $_____ $_____

8

Starting a New Business

You may conclude that counseling a buyer on starting a new business is not good business practice on your part. After all, you can't earn a commission. You may decide, however, that if your potential buyer is going to look at this alternative, you will be better off if you are involved. You may help your potential buyer avoid some pitfalls and do a better job of evaluating this alternative.

If you believe that providing good service pays off in the long run, be sure that you are capable of knowledgeably discussing what is involved in starting a new business.

WHY YOUR BUYERS SHOULD CONSIDER THE ALTERNATIVE

Starting a new business may sometimes be a better alternative than buying an existing one for a number of reasons. Two are that it can be cheaper, faster, and less complicated, and it can result in a business that matches your buyer's criteria exactly. Some businesses, particularly service businesses, are easy to start. Consulting practices, real-estate sales companies, repair services, small restaurants, and professional service practices (accounting, legal, financial, medical) can all be started without great difficulty, although they may take time to grow, and an individual still may come out ahead by buying.

If your buyer has a unique idea or some special personal advantage, he or she may have a good reason to start a new business. A special personal advantage might be a patent, a location, or a ready-made client/customer base. He or she may have a one-of-a-kind source of supply or some special relationships that will ostensibly insure success. Another reason is price. Sometimes, the type of business your buyer wants to buy may not be affordable. In the case of a unique idea—a new product or service, say—there may be no alternative because no such companies exist. More often, there are companies that closely match your buyer's criteria, but they are either beyond your buyer's financial capability or just not for sale.

One of the negatives of starting a new business is the higher risk exposure. "Six out of every ten new businesses fail within the first five years." This unproven but often-quoted statistic shouldn't surprise you. A business that has survived five years has proven that its products, prices, location, and methods of operation are at least acceptable to its market. These key components in the start-up business are all unproven. The new business plan may be to get positive cash flow in one year, but it may take two. The business may need to have enough cash to keep going for much longer than planned. A new business owner may find that some part of the business plan is more difficult to attain than anticipated. Perhaps developing new customers takes more selling skills than he or she possesses, or maybe hiring employees turns out to cost more and take more time.

Under-capitalization and lack of required skills are the two major reasons for new business failure. Both are the result of the high uncertainty in business start-ups. A profitable, cash-generating, existing business may cost a premium to buy, but it may have earned it.

THE PROCESS

Starting a business involves three things: a marketable idea, a plan, and the resources to carry out the plan.

THE IDEA

The idea for the new business need not be a new idea or even your buyer's idea, but it does have to be a marketable idea. Here are some questions to pose:

- Does the idea address a real need or want? Is there, or could there be, a demand?

- Will the demand be big enough to support a business? Is the field open or crowded with competition?

- Can the idea actually be transformed into a business? Is the technology available? Will the cost result in a product or service price that the market will bear?

- Does your buyer have the knowledge and skills required? Has anyone else tried this idea? What was the outcome and why?

Answering these questions takes much thought, a lot of research, and, very often, some intuition.

Research is a sometimes-maligned activity in new business development. While it's true that research has killed some good ideas, it has killed far more bad ones. Intuition, or gut feeling, has launched many a business that has not remained afloat. Using both research and intuition makes obvious good sense. Even if your buyer has overwhelming gut feelings about his or her idea, bankers or the venture capital firm or, for that matter, relatives, if they are lending or investing, will want answers to some of those questions. Even if no one else asks the questions, anyone starting a business should ask them themselves and do the research to answer them. Why neglect what's available? One can always reject the answers in favor of intuition.

In the end, anyone starting a business will have to use intuition to pass judgment on the idea, anyway. Research and analysis can spot extremes and raise warnings, but at best they will provide only estimates and probabilities. The individual must decide.

THE PLAN

The plan for a new business will be a paradox. It is based on projections and conjecture. There is no historic pattern or experience base to use as a guide, yet, the new business plan is expected to be exceedingly detailed. Here is a plan outline:

1. *General concept statement.* The business idea may not be obvious to anyone else. If the founder expects others to be financial or human resources, these people must be provided with a succinct description. The concept statement should describe the idea and summarize its potential risks and rewards.

2. *The product or service.* Define the product or service. Show costs for varying levels of production. Try to show the name and the packaging, if any. Explain any uniqueness or competitive advantage. Describe any protection for the product or service. Define the barriers others would face in entering the field.

3. *The market.* Define the market in several ways:
   - Size
   - Composition/segments
   - Growth
   - Location
   - Demographics
   - Competition

   Describe how the buying decision for the product or service is made and who makes it. Present the pricing rationale. Describe the competitive environment. Explain any special features about the market, such as distribution methods, cyclicality, government impact, and so on.

4. *The organization.* The first organizational issue is the legal form of organization. Figure 2–1 in chapter 2 contains a description of the various forms and the considerations for selecting one over another. The individual's attorney and accountant should give guidance on this choice. The second organizational issue relates to the structure and the people planned for the new business. Any investor or lender will consider it vital to know how the founder and his or her associates are qualified to succeed. Resumes and references will be required.

5. *The schedule of events.* Prepare a detailed schedule of all the events that are involved in bringing the new business on stream. The schedule should show *what* the event is; *when* it occurs,

including, if it's appropriate, when it begins and ends; and *who* is responsible for each event. No list can be complete, but here is a sample of the kinds of events to schedule:

a. Completing the design of the product or service and its packaging

b. Selecting suppliers

c. Hiring employees

d. Choosing a location

e. Developing brochures

f. Creating advertising and promotion programs

g. Obtaining licenses and permits

h. Setting up special announcement meetings

i. Scheduling customer contacts

j. Setting up shop—furniture, telephones, tools, computers, supplies, etc.

k. Selecting distributors

l. Establishing controls and measurement check points

THE BUDGET

Your buyer can use several of the worksheets in this book to help set up a budget:

1. Worksheet 5A: How much money you need (your personal budget—Chapter 6)

2. Worksheet 6: Sources of money (a personal balance sheet and a list of sources of money—Chapter 7)

3. Worksheet 9: Income statement format (a format for budgeting income and expenses—Chapter 9)

4. Worksheet 10: Balance sheet format (a format to project your assets and liabilities—Chapter 9)

5. Worksheet 11: Sources and applications of funds format (a format to show the flow of funds in and out of the business—Chapter 9)

6. Worksheet 7: Business start-up budget format (a more detailed, *monthly* breakdown of income, costs, expenses, and cash flow—Chapter 8)

Any new business has two special concerns that the budget must address: cash flow and early warnings of trouble. Worksheet 7 is broken down into monthly detail to give a close look at these two key concerns. Anyone starting a business should learn quickly which weekly or daily indicators can give even earlier warnings.

Cash flow is doubly important for the new business. Not only will your buyer/founder have to deal with the uncertainty of a start-up business budget, but, in all likelihood, he or she has had to put personal and household finances on a matching budget. Advise your buyer to integrate these two budgets to get a complete picture of his or her cash situation. Finally, because start-ups have so much uncertainty, advise your buyer to prepare a contingency budget. The contingency budget should reflect a "worst-case" situation where cash flow would be at its reasonably poorest level. Integrating this worst-case contingency budget with the personal budget will point out potential problems and give an opportunity to make judgments about your plan. A business start-up budget format is shown as Worksheet 7 at the end of this chapter.

THE RESOURCES

The *resources* to help start a business include financial resources, physical resources, and information and advice. These resources are not always easy to find or convenient to use. People starting new businesses need to be downright ingenious in recognizing and utilizing everything that can help them complete the extraordinarily difficult task of starting a business.

Financial Resources

Chapter 7 presented an array of financing alternatives. Figure 7–1 of that chapter provides a summary. The sources are relevant for start-ups with one major exception: There is no seller financing. The basic source of money for buying a business is not available to the start-up business.

Physical Resources

A major objective of most start-up businesses is to keep costs low. Physical resources can represent a large part of start-up costs and need special attention. Here are some ideas you can pass on to your buyer:

1. *Lease or rent rather than buy.* Of course, the lease vs. buy decision has to make basic financial sense, but those starting a business should be looking for ways to avoid large purchases by renting what they need.

2. *Keep the scale small and avoid extravagances.* Investigate secondhand equipment and furniture when practical. If only a small amount of space is needed, find out if there are any "incubator" type facilities in the area. These are typically facilities sponsored by a development agency or academic institution to aid start-up ventures by providing very small scale facilities and, often, shared support systems.

3. *Borrow or share where possible.* The easiest opportunity for sharing is with office space. But many others exist for those who have the courage to ask for help. People tend to admire the entrepreneur starting a new business; they are willing to help.

Information and Advice

This resource is abundant to the point of excess. Figure 9–2 in the next chapter lists 31 sources of information, most of which are applicable to a business start-up. Start-ups don't require the intense advice and support of the negotiations and the purchase of a business. But there are a host of details—setting up the books, getting tax identification numbers, obtaining licenses and permits—that will require advisors' help.

THE MOST IMPORTANT RESOURCE

The founder's time is the single most important resource in the business start-up. This book has made the point that nothing happens in business transactions unless someone makes it happen. This concept is even more important to the start-up process. There are no employees to give assistance; no long-standing bankers, vendors, and suppliers to provide support; and no established customers to offer encouragement.

It is the founder who must create and build the enthusiasm that will attract others to the idea and to the business. In the beginning, the founder will have the only vision of the business and the only stake in its success.

Business Start-Up Budget

A. MONTHLY PROFIT AND LOSS STATEMENT

	Month 1	Month 2	Month 3	Month 4	Month 5	Month 6	Month 7	Month 8	Month 9	Month 10	Month 11	Month 12	Total
Sales													
Cost of sales													
Gross profit													
Expenses													
Owner's salary													
Owner's benefits and taxes													
No. of people													
Employee salaries													
Employee benefits and taxes													
Rent													
Utilities													
Travel and entertainment													
Selling expenses													
Depreciation													
Insurance													
Supplies													
Interest													
Automobile													
Dues, licenses, subscriptions													

	Month 1	Month 2	Month 3	Month 4	Month 5	Month 6	Month 7	Month 8	Month 9	Month 10	Month 11	Month 12	Total
Legal and accounting													
Other													
Other													
Other													
Total Expenses													
Pretax profit													

B. CASH FLOW PROJECTIONS

	Month 1	Month 2	Month 3	Month 4	Month 5	Month 6	Month 7	Month 8	Month 9	Month 10	Month 11	Month 12	Total
Cash on hand													
Cash in bank													
Near cash investments													
Cash balance beginning													
Cash added													
Cash sales													
Collections from accounts receivable													
Interest investment income													
Loans to the business													
Other													
Total cash added													
Total Cash Available													
Cash Expenses													
Purchases of materials & equipment													

	Month 1	Month 2	Month 3	Month 4	Month 5	Month 6	Month 7	Month 8	Month 9	Month 10	Month 11	Month 12	Total
Salaries and benefits													
Rent													
Utilities													
Travel and entertainment													
Selling expenses													
Insurance													
Suppliers													
Interest													
Automobile													
Dues, licenses, subscriptions													
Legal and accounting													
Other													
Other													
Other													
Repayment of loan principal													
Taxes													
Total Cash Paid Out													
Cash Balance Ending													
Cash Flow (Deficit) Month													
Cash Flow (Deficit) Cumulative													

Reprinted from *How to Leave Your Job and Buy A Business of Your Own* by C. D. Peterson, published by the McGraw-Hill Book Company. Copyright © 1988 McGraw-Hill, Inc. Reprinted with permission.

CHAPTER 9

Analyzing the Business

You will need the skills to analyze a business, not only for your own understanding, but to be able to present the business, overcome objections, and more often than not, help the buyer.

This chapter will present the analysis of a business with the buyer in mind. This is not to assume or propose any conflict of interest on your part. Your loyalty is to your client, who is usually the seller. However, the only way to present the process of analysis is through the buyer's eyes. Furthermore, you need to be skilled in the same techniques as the buyer in order to properly advise your client. Finally, you will sometimes end up showing buyers how to undertake an analysis. It is strongly advocated that you do not *perform* the analysis or advise the buyer on the conclusions. Remind the buyer that you represent the seller, and let the buyer rely on his or her own accountant for financial analysis and advice. By this point in the process you should have a "Confidential Receipt of Information" form signed by the buyer (See Appendix B).

MANAGING ADVISORS

The three advisors most involved in analyzing businesses are accountants, attorneys, and intermediaries. If there is another broker or intermediary, you, the buyer, and the seller need to be certain of that person's loyalty and responsibility. Get a clear definition of his or her function.

INTERMEDIARIES

Some intermediaries have full power to negotiate, whereas others are only communication conduits. Some are active and creative in structuring deals, and some only transmit offers. Levels of skill and experience vary. Ask how the other intermediary operates. Find out how the clients expect things to proceed. Another intermediary may be very helpful to the process; however, you need to know the role played by any other broker or intermediary as part of managing this final phase of the process.

ACCOUNTANTS

Managing the accountants begins with determining what kind of arrangements the parties will have with them. By this time, the accountants should be well aware of their clients' objectives and resources.

Unless buyers are secure in their own skills, they will want their accountants to perform tests and analyses and provide them with recommendations. They and their accountants should discuss the limitations of using accounting-statement and tax-return information and the risks of using adjusted information such as will most often be used in analyzing small businesses. Both kinds of information are needed, and they have to agree on how best to use them. Buyers may want their accountants to advise on how to structure the transaction. Whatever the relationship is between the buyer and his or her accountant, it should be made clear, including how fees will be charged.

You should be aware of a special dilemma that accountants face when advising on the purchase of a business. If a buyer relies heavily on an accountant and buys a business on which the accountant has favorably advised and then has trouble (even of the buyer's own making), he or she might hold the accountant liable. If, on the other hand, the client buys a business that the accountant has advised against and the business is successful, the accountant has only to rejoice in the client's success. Therefore, there may be pressure on the accountant to avoid positive recommendations. A buyer can avoid applying that pressure by letting the accountant know that he or she welcomes advice from advisors in making the final decision, but accepts responsibility for the outcome once that decision has been made.

ATTORNEYS

Managing attorneys involves much of the same. The buyer and the attorney(s) should have a discussion about how they will work together. The buyer may want the attorney to review just the contract and closing documents or may want him or her to handle the negotiations completely. In between these extremes are requests for advice and counsel on the purchase transaction. If the buyer has already selected the company he or she is going after, the attorney might be able to estimate the complexity of the transaction and thereby determine how much in time and charges the buyer should budget.

The last step in managing accountants and attorneys is to develop a team approach. Their work is interrelated. For example, how this purchase will impact on the buyer's total tax situation requires their coordination. Estate planning is another area of common interest. These two advisors can be excellent resources in developing nego-tiating tactics. The buyer's objective—buying a business—should become their objective.

EVALUATING THE BUSINESS

Gathering information and analyzing all the factors surrounding a business can seem like an overwhelming task for the buyer. Just remind the buyer that he or she does *not* have to do the analysis alone. And most assuredly, it doesn't have to be done in a hurry. While the analysis should be conducted with consideration for the time of others, it should not be rushed. You and the buyer have access to accountants and attorneys as advisors, and you can find specialized advisors if you need them. Yet, with all this help, any final decision to buy or sell will be made on imperfect and incomplete information because there is no other. Buying a business is a risk. The challenge is to minimize the risk as best as possible.

One constraint in the evaluation activities is the need for confidentiality. It was mentioned in Chapter 4 that the concern for confidentiality by the seller is genuine. It should be the buyer's concern, too. If knowledge of the potential sale of the business upsets customers, employees, the landlord, or others, it may put the deal in jeopardy. Telling a friend or neighbor about the deal may spread the news to the entire community. This requirement for confidentiality means that extra care should be taken when gathering information.

This complex task of evaluation can be broken into steps. First, determine *what* information is needed. Then consider *where* the information might be found. Finally, work on *how* to analyze the information that you and the buyer uncover.

THE INFORMATION NEEDED

As mentioned in Chapter 4 in the discussion of listings, much of this information will be obtained at the time the listing is taken. To review that list, Figure 4–6 is repeated here as Figure 9–1. Now, however, you will not be limited to the seller as your only source of information. Finding the information is the next task.

THE INFORMATION SOURCES

The seller will still be the primary source of information, but you do not have to rely on that source alone. Figure 9–2 is a list of 31 different sources of information. Not all will be relevant to the candidate company, but you may find some surprisingly good ones in the list.

You and the buyer can locate all but a few of these sources on your own. The rest you can reach by working with your advisors. Some sleuthing should yield the information you and the buyer are seeking (and more). Now that you have it, you need to decide what the information means.

The owner's reason for selling
Company history
The company's purpose, what it does
People
Organization
Facilities
Equipment
Technology
Market
Competition
Company operations:
    Manufacturing
    Legal
    Marketing and sales
    Accounting and finance
    General strengths and weaknesses
    Outside factors
    Financial performance*

* Some business buyers and analysts pay relatively little attention to past financial performance and give more weight to financial projections of future performance.

Figure 9–1. What Information Is Needed

The seller	The intermediary
Company records	Tax returns
Associations	Franchise records
Competitors	Employees (and former employees)
Consultants	Banks
Suppliers	Government records
Seller's advisors	Your advisors
Newspapers and magazines	Library
Neighboring businesses	Your networks
Chamber of Commerce	Better Business Bureau
Court/land records	Landlord
Unions	Bonding company
Patent office	Credit reporting companies
Insurance policies and agents	Stockbroker
Real-estate broker	Private investigator

and your own personal observation

Figure 9–2. Sources of Information

INTERPRETING THE INFORMATION

You are first faced with the task of sorting through all the data you and the buyer have gathered and then organizing it. There is a "Company Profile Data Form" in Appendix C to help you organize and record your information. It also helps you match the facts about a company to the requirements the buyers will have, requirements such as risk and the criteria for buying a business. Part of the "Company Profile Data Form" will be shown at the end of this chapter as Worksheet 8.

The *qualitative* process of analysis you will use is called *forced rating*. It is simply a 1-to-10 or 1-to-6 scale that forces you and the buyer to rate your findings explicitly. The *quantitative* portion of the process will be conventional financial analysis.

When you took the listing, you gathered information on some or all of 17 business factors. As a summary and reminder, here they are:

- History
- People
- Facilities
- Technology
- Competition
- Legal
- Accounting and finance
- Outside factors
- Financial performance
- Purpose
- Organization
- Equipment
- Market(s)
- Manufacturing
- Marketing and sales
- General
- Reason for selling

Worksheet 8 will help you assist your buyer in rating the combined weight of these factors against the buyer's criteria and risk elements. The forced rating process does two things:

1. It forms an integrated idea of desirability.
2. It points out extremes and suggests areas for further investigation.

The rating is imperfect because it assumes an equal value for each criterion and for each risk factor. Nonetheless, you have followed a logical path to this point in helping your buyer make first judgments about whether this business is for him or her. If the business is far outside the preferred degree of risk or does not satisfy the criteria at all, there is no need for the buyer to analyze the quantitative data. If, however, this judgment does not eliminate the candidate, move on to the numbers.

QUANTITATIVE ANALYSIS

What follows is an overview of fairly conventional financial analysis. The level of the buyer's own skills in this area and the complexity of the data will dictate to what the extent an accountant should be involved.

COMPARATIVE ANALYSIS

As the name implies, *comparative analysis* involves comparison. Facts, figures, and ratios developed for the business the buyer is considering are compared with standards of some kind. The most readily available standards are the company's previous financial statements. Comparing current and historic financial performance is a sure way to spot significant deviations in current performance. Comparisons can also use more or less generally accepted benchmarks, such as a 2-to-1 ratio between current assets and current liabilities. An accountant or banker can provide you and the buyer with these interesting but very imprecise rules of thumb.

Other comparisons can be made with industry norms. Basic financial figures and ratios are available for many kinds and sizes of business. Industry trade associations may publish them. Trade papers and magazines sometimes publish an annual edition of financial performance ratios. Stockbrokers have access to performance statistics for many kinds of businesses. The government offers industry financial statistics through the SBA and the Department of Commerce. Two comprehensive sources of ratios are *The Almanac of Business and Industrial Ratios* and *Financial Studies of the Small Business.**

Almanac of Business and Industrial Financial Ratios, by Leo Troy, Prentice-Hall, Inc., Englewood Cliffs, NJ; *Financial Studies of the Small Business*, Financial Research Associates, Winter Haven, FL.

FINANCIAL STATEMENT ANALYSIS

A second kind of quantitative analysis, *financial statement analysis*, involves the interpretation of the financial statement contents. Here, instead of comparing, you are trying to understand and evaluate.

Both kinds of quantitative analyses—comparison and financial statement analysis—are based on ratios, turnover rates, return rates, percentage analyses, sensitivity analyses, break-even analyses, and an analysis of the sources and application of funds (cash).

Ratio Analysis

Ratio analysis is a common quantitative technique. The relationship between two financial statement items can be reduced to a simple standardized ratio that is easy to compare and understand. Here are some common ratios and their implications:

1. *Current Ratio*. This is the ratio of current assets to current liabilities:

$$\frac{\text{Current Assets}}{\text{Current Liabilities}} = \text{Current Ratio}$$

It's an indicator of a company's ability to meet its short-term obligations. It is an indicator of liquid strength, at least in the short term.

2. *The Acid Test Ratio*. It is an even more stringent liquidity measure. It also uses the ratio between current assets and current liabilities, but inventory and other nonliquid assets are removed from the current asset category:

$$\frac{\text{Liquid Current Assets}}{\text{Current Liabilities}} = \text{Acid Test Ratio}$$

3. *Fixed Assets to Long-term Liabilities*. Although this is not a much used test in small businesses, it does show the degree of security behind the long-term debt:

$$\frac{\text{Fixed Assets}}{\text{Long-Term Liabilities}} = \text{Long-term Debt Coverage}$$

4. *Turnover.* The two common ratios are inventory and accounts receivable turnover. They are good comparative measures to help analyze how well the candidate company does in managing these two asset investments.

Inventory turnover is typically calculated by dividing the cost of goods by the average inventory:

$$\frac{\text{Net Sales}}{\text{Average Inventory}} = \text{Inventory Turnover}$$

Accounts receivable turnover is determined by dividing net sales by average receivables:

$$\frac{\text{Net Sales}}{\text{Average Receivables}} = \text{Average Receivables Turnover}$$

5. *Return on Investment (ROI).* In this book, return on investment is computed using the adjusted owner's cash flow as the return figure and the net market value of the investment as the investment figure:

$$\frac{\text{Adjusted Owner's Cash Flow}}{\text{Net Investment}} = \text{ROI}$$

These measures are used because they produce information useful in making an investment decision. However, to be able to compare the candidate company to conventional standards of return on investment, you will need to use conventional measures. The conventional measures vary from industry to industry, and it is vital that you and the buyer understand them. The return on investment in industries with large capital investments will bear no comparison to returns in certain service industries. For example, when analyzing residential real-estate companies, the return on investment is a secondary measure. The analyses are more often expressed in terms of percentage of net revenue (company dollar). Just determine how the standard is derived for the industry you are examining and use the same method of calculation.

Return percentages are a critical part of the analysis because they reduce all of the financial data to one key number. Because of the apparent precision employed in computing the return percentage, there is a tendency to misuse it. It is a good comparative measure (if the standard of comparison is valid) but not a good valuative measure. The percentage return on investment is not a measure of return on *actual cash* investment unless all cash was invested.

Return on investment has one other practical shortcoming. It does not measure any appreciation the investment may have enjoyed. The following real-estate investment example can demonstrate these shortcomings (ignore any tax implications):

If you bought a small shopping center for $1 million and after all expenses you received income of $25,000, you would have a gross ROI of 2–1/2 percent. But if you only put $100,000 in cash as a down payment, you could view your "cash-on-cash" ROI as 25 percent.

Assume further that after a year you sell the shopping center for $1.1 million. Does that $100,000 profit represent a 10 percent return on the $1 million, or does it represent a 100 percent return on the $100,000 cash you actually invested? In fact, it is both. Remember that the actual amount of $100,000 is the same, only your definition of *investment* (the degree of financing) changed.

Be aware of two principles of financing that apply to this part of the analysis:

1. A high level of financing can make a bad business affordable, but it doesn't make it a good business.

2. The basic rule of financing says that you borrow only if you can earn more than it costs you to borrow. If a buyer puts down very little cash and borrows a great deal, he or she may end up using all the income from the business for debt repayments.

These two principles mean that this very important analysis of return on investment needs to involve not only the historic financial statement rates of return but the future projections of returns based on your buyer's financing plan.

Cost and Expense Analysis

This form of analysis can be very enlightening because it allows you and your buyer to compare your target company with others, with its own history, and with your own judgment. The analysis is done by dividing sales by the individual cost and expense items. Here is a simplified example:

Item	Amount	Percent of Sales
Sales	$700,000	100
Cost of goods	315,000	45
Gross profit	385,000	55
Salaries	84,000	12
Rent	35,000	5
Utilities	14,000	2
Interest	21,000	3
Selling expenses	35,000	5
Administration	42,000	6
Transportation	14,000	2
Total expenses	$245,000	35
Pretax profit	$140,000	20

Be alert for changes in trends and numbers that seem outside the normal standards and outside your common-sense idea of what is normal.

Sensitivity Analysis

As the name suggests, this quantitative analysis attempts to determine how sensitive the company's performance is to changes in income, costs, and expenses. The analysis is accomplished by posing "what if" questions:

- What if the rent doubles?
- What if I add two people?
- What if sales go up/down 5 percent?
- What if I raise prices 10 percent and lose 1 percent in volume?

The objective is to get a feel for where the business is most vulnerable and where it has the most potential.

Break-Even Analysis

This is a special form of sensitivity analysis that allows you to better understand the relationships among sales, fixed costs, variable costs, and profit. It assumes that some costs—such as rent, administration, and insurance—are more or less fixed in the short term, while other costs—such as the cost of materials and selling commissions—vary with volume. After deciding whether the cost or expense is fixed or variable, you construct a chart similar to the one in Figure 9–3. This will give you an idea of what volume of business needs to be done in order to begin making a profit.

This is a particularly useful analysis for testing or verifying a seller's claims. For example, if a seller claims that all a business needs is a little attention to sales—when, in fact, the problem is high fixed overhead—this type of analysis can be very revealing. It will show just how much of an increase in sales would be required to improve profitability.

Sources and Application of Funds

This analysis will show you, for a specific period of time, whether the company the buyer is considering consumed more or less cash than it generated. The analysis uses a comparison between the balance sheets of two periods and information from the income statement.

The income statement has two items that affect the analysis: profit (or loss) and noncash expenditures, such as depreciation. Profit and depreciation are sources of funds. The simple rules to follow with the balance sheet are:

- An increase in assets is a use of funds.
- A decrease in assets is a source of funds.
- An increase in liabilities is a source of funds.
- A decrease in liabilities is a use of funds.

If the company the buyer is considering has professionally prepared statements, they normally will include a statement of sources and application of funds.

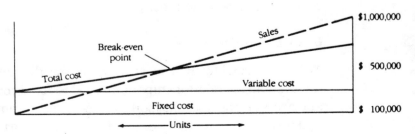

Figure 9–3. Break-even Analysis

HELP IN ANALYZING THE INFORMATION

You and the buyer have several sources for help in analyzing the information you have gathered. Advisors, industry statistics and standards, and company history are some that have been discussed. Real-estate appraisers, inventory appraisal companies, specialized equipment appraisers, and dealers are others who can help (the Resources Literature section at the back of this book lists several useful books).

THE SELLER'S ADVISORS

You will also use the seller and the seller's advisors. No one knows more about the business than they. Often the only way to understand some fact or figure is to ask the seller. Some sellers are candid to the point of total disclosure. The obvious risk to a buyer in asking these sources is that they are the seller's and they want to present the best picture possible. Offsetting that risk is the fact that the seller is probably going to finance the purchase. Sellers know that if buyers discover they have been deceived, they will be less cooperative in repaying their debt. Do as you would with any advice and evaluate the source as well as the information.

You and the buyer may have to persuade the seller to let you use one special source of help, but it is worth the effort. The seller's banker will know more about the business than almost anyone. If you have the chance, recommend the seller's banker to be the buyer's banker. The motive for working with this source of help is even greater then. The seller's banker will be less likely to use puffery to help the sale and will be interested in seeing a well-executed transaction.

THE COMPUTER

A recent source of help is computer-assisted analysis. Several software programs on the market can calculate ratios, construct comparative tables, and provide projections of sales, profit, and cash flow based on your plans.

The computer is also most helpful in doing sensitivity analyses. These are the analyses that pose "What if" questions. The computer, and its software program, have the capability of calculating the total impact of particular changes in the company ("What if sales increase or decrease by 5 percent?"). The calculations are done so quickly that you can probe nearly every variable.

Three format worksheets are provided to help you and the buyer capture data for your analyses:

1. Worksheet 9: Income Statement Format
2. Worksheet 10: Balance Sheet Format
3. Worksheet 11: Source and Application of Funds Format

RECONSIDERATION

At some point, the buyer will decide he or she has gathered enough knowledge to make a decision on whether to reject the candidate or proceed to make an offer. Before proceeding, the buyer should take the time to reconsider the whole idea of owning a business. Suggest that he or she go back to Worksheet 3 and re-evaluate whether his or her level of satisfaction will be significantly improved if he or she buys the business under consideration. Compare life situations under the following two assumptions: the buyer owns this business, or he or she has a realistic job. Use a "plus and minus" list. If appropriate, involve the buyer's spouse and family.

COMPARE INCOME

Comparing the income from a job with the income from the business requires that you make some assumptions about the perquisites the buyer will afford himself or herself. Any generous fringe benefits that might come from employment need to be carefully evaluated. Pension considerations may be important in your buyer's situation. Employment of family members and the buyer's personal tax situation will have an influence on this comparison.

COMPARE WEALTH

Projecting the buyer's wealth may be difficult, but it is important to do. The method to follow is to compare the buyer's total balance sheet under the same two assumptions of business ownership or employment. Have the buyer prepare a personal balance sheet that reflects the present situation. Then have the buyer prepare a balance sheet that projects total assets and liabilities under the most probable assumptions about the performance of the business. Try to have the buyer do the projection for one year and for five years. Repeat the projection of the balance sheet assuming that the buyer has a job instead of the business.

COMPARE SATISFACTION

The buyer can only imagine some of the satisfactions and frustrations that will come from owning the business, so the comparison with employment, though necessary, is very subjective. Have the buyer make the comparison by thinking through the things that impact on satisfaction: family consideration, freedom, stress, risk, independence, working hours and conditions, intellectual stimulation, status and image, security—both short term and long term—recognition, accomplishment, and the special element of obligation.

The obligations that come with business ownership might be viewed as the weight to be placed on the balance scale opposite the feelings of impotence experienced by the employee. When working for others, people are, de facto, subordinate. No matter how benign or abusive the treatment, people are subject to being told what to do and are directly dependent on others whom they cannot avoid. When a person owns a business, he or she automatically incurs obligations. The obligations are legal, financial, and in some cases, psychological. They exist 24 hours a day and are unavoidable—when you own a business, you can't just quit at 5 o'clock.

If your buyer has alternatives other than owning a business or having a job—such as teaching, consulting, retirement, or government service—include these alternatives in this reconsideration.

WORKSHEET 8

A. Rating versus your business buying criteria (see Chapter 3 for review). Use 1-to-10 scale; 10 is best.

Cash flow	_____	Growth potential	_____
Location	_____	Working conditions	_____
Liquidity	_____	Status and image	_____
People intensity	_____	Competition	_____
Overall desirability	_____	Content of the business	_____

Total _____ ÷ 10 = _____ Rating

B. Risk evaluation (see Chapter 4 for review). Use 1-to-6 scale; 6 is low risk.

Company history	_____	Special skills required	_____
The industry segment	_____	Special relationships required	_____
Location	_____	Labor situation	_____
Return *of* investment	_____	Management situation	_____
Return *on* investment	_____	Outside dependency	_____
Company reputation	_____	Products and services	_____
Competition	_____	Franchises/licenses required	_____
Technology	_____	Legal exposure	_____

Total _____ ÷ 16 = _____ Rating

Reprinted from *How to Leave Your Job and Buy A Business of Your Own* by C. D. Peterson, published by the McGraw-Hill Book Company. Copyright © 1988 McGraw-Hill, Inc. Reprinted with permission.

WORKSHEET 9

Income Statement (P&L) Format

For the period _____ to _____

Sales:		$_____
Cost of sales	$_____	
Gross Profit		$_____
Expenses:		
Owner's salary		$_____
Owner's benefits and taxes		_____
Employee salaries (no. of people ____)		_____
Employee benefits and taxes		_____
Rent		_____
Utilities		_____
Travel and entertainment		_____
Selling expenses		_____
Depreciation		_____
Insurance		_____
Supplies		_____
Interest		_____
Automobile		_____
Dues, licenses, subscriptions		_____
Legal and accounting		_____
Other _____		_____
Other _____		_____
Other _____		_____
Total expenses		$_____
Pretax Profit		$_____

WORKSHEET 10

Balance Sheet Format

as of _____

Assets

Current Assets:
Cash .... $_____
Accounts receivable .... _____
Notes receivable .... _____
Inventory .... _____
Prepaid expenses .... _____
Other .... _____
Total Current Assets .... $_____

Fixed Assets:
Furniture, fixtures, machinery, and equipment $_____
Less: accumulated depreciation   _____ $_____

Land and buildings   _____
Less: accumulated depreciation   _____ $_____

Total Fixed Assets .... $_____
Other assets _____ .... _____
Total Assets .... $_____

Liabilities and Owner's Equity

Current Liabilities:
Accounts payable .... $_____
Wages payable .... _____
Taxes payable .... _____
Interest payable .... _____
Notes leases (current portion) .... _____
Services or products owed to customers .... _____
Other liabilities .... _____
Total Current Liabilities .... $_____

Long-term Liabilities:
Notes .... $_____
Mortgages .... _____
Other _____ .... _____
Total Long-term Liabilities .... $_____

Owner's Equity:
Capital stock .... $_____
Retained earnings .... _____
Total Liabilities and Owner's Equity .... $_____

Reprinted from *How to Leave Your Job and Buy A Business of Your Own* by C. D. Peterson, published by the McGraw-Hill Book Company. Copyright © 1988 McGraw-Hill, Inc. Reprinted with permission.

WORKSHEET 11

Sources and Application of Funds Format

Funds Received from:

Profits	$_____
Noncash expenses (i.e., depreciation)	_____
Increases in liabilities	_____
Decreases in assets (other than depreciation)	_____
Added equity	_____
Total Funds Received	$_____

Funds Applied to:

Losses	$_____
Increases in assets	_____
Decreases in liabilities	_____
Payout of profit (dividends)	_____
Total Funds Applied	$_____

Reprinted from *How to Leave Your Job and Buy A Business of Your Own* by C. D. Peterson, published by the McGraw-Hill Book Company. Copyright © 1988 McGraw-Hill, Inc. Reprinted with permission.

10

If the Business Is a Franchise

Franchises offer some special appeals, particularly to the first-time business owner. Most come with tested systems to help manage the business. From the sign over the front door to the payroll accounting system, the franchisee has the franchiser's experience and support available. Many established franchisers have field consultants who visit the locations on a regular basis and when called to help with problems.

A common expression used to describe owning a franchise is "being in business for yourself but not by yourself." Owning a franchise can transform the buyer instantly into a part of a large organization with sophisticated advertising and strong market recognition.

Buying a franchise is a fairly straightforward proposition. Federal and state laws require the franchiser to disclose the material facts about the franchise and the offer to sell. There is little or no negotiating. This is considerably different from buying an established, nonfranchised business where financial data may be vague and the price is determined only after lengthy negotiations. The franchise industry enjoys a better reputation than in years past and is growing rapidly, as shown in Figure 10–1. The super successes in the field,

It is estimated that, by the end of the century, half the retail sales in the United States will be made through franchised outlets.

	1970	1987 EST.	% Growth
Number of Establishments	396,000	500,000	+26
Dollars Sales	$120 billion	$625 billion	+420
Employment	2.5 million	6.3 million	+152

Figure 10–1. The Growth of Franchising

such as McDonald's, coupled with tight government regulation and policing by the industry itself, have raised the image of franchises. While there are still bad franchises and dishonorable franchisers, franchise ownership is generally viewed more positively than in the past.

Franchises are now available in a wide variety of types and prices. One recent collection of franchise offerings contained a $3,000 franchise to provide business education seminars and a $1-million top-name restaurant franchise. In between were franchises for instant printing ($35,000) hair styling ($75,000), automotive repair ($100,000), and even a basketball franchise ($250,000). All this variety means that people have a better chance of finding opportunities that match their desires and their financial capabilities, thus making franchises attractive and affordable to more people who are seeking to become entrepreneurs.

WHAT IS A FRANCHISE?

A *franchise* is a license. In most cases, it is a license to use a franchiser's name and to offer its products or services for sale in exchange for certain fees. The terms of the license are spelled out in a *franchise agreement*.

THE FRANCHISE AGREEMENT

The franchise agreement will cover in detail the obligations the franchisee (buyer) and the franchiser have to each other:

1. *The price of the franchise, the terms of any financing, and the ongoing royalty schedule.*

2. *A list of exactly what the franchisee is getting for the money.* In addition to the right to use the franchiser's name and to sell the products or services, the franchisee may be getting training, certain equipment, a starting inventory, special promotions, or a number of other things.

3. *The procedures that must be followed in operating the franchise.* Some franchises have very detailed manuals that cover all aspects of operations, from what color uniforms are required to how to clean the floors. Some franchises permit a degree of flexibility; others require strict adherence to procedures. All require some form of reporting and controls.

4. *The duration of the agreement and the procedures governing sale, renewal, and transfer.* Also covered are the conditions under which either side may cancel the agreement.

5. *A definition of the territory.* The territory may be narrow or broad, exclusive or unprotected, or some combination that might even change over time.

6. *A definition of the responsibilities for operations.* The agreement covers the responsibility for pricing, purchasing, advertising, paying invoices, hiring, training, insurance coverage, maintenance, security, and similar items. Some franchisers require the franchisee to personally operate their franchise. If the franchiser provides consulting or troubleshooting support, it should be covered in the agreement.

7. *The plan for the facility.* Some franchisers provide the complete facility, others give detailed specifications, and others offer little or no guidance. Some franchisers own the facility and lease it to the franchisee. In other cases, the facility is rented from a landlord—sometimes from the franchisee.

The franchise agreement is an imposing and important document that should be reviewed by the franchisee's attorney.

THE PLUSES OF OWNING A FRANCHISE

The most obvious benefit derived from owning a franchise is an established, tested product or service. Equally important can be the methods and systems that have been refined to a smooth set of procedures and that proved successful in the marketplace. Franchisees benefit from the franchiser's learning curve. Also, the powerful franchiser is almost certainly able to secure a better location than an individual. The franchiser has more technical expertise in site selection and has more financial clout to negotiate and capture good locations.

If the franchiser is a heavy advertiser and promoter, the recognition factor can be a big plus for the franchisee. The economy of scale available to the franchiser can permit advertising on television and other media too expensive for the independent operator. Economies of scale may extend to the purchase of materials and supplies, giving franchisees lower prices than they could obtain on their own.

Training, consulting, and any other kinds of help the franchiser provides can be very meaningful. The independent operator has limited and often expensive resources to turn to for help. The buyer may appreciate the availability of the franchiser's field staff.

THE MINUSES OF OWNING A FRANCHISE

The restrictions and controls imposed by the franchiser are the greatest drawbacks to a franchised business.

The license fee and ongoing royalties can seem onerous, particularly if franchiser support is weak. The ownership of the franchise license is not permanent. This could pose a serious problem later on, especially if the owner wants to sell or bequeath the business. The franchiser's management and financial strength may become weak or may fail. Franchisees can be adversely affected by events outside their control. They may be prohibited from expanding or relocating their business because of the franchiser's licensing of others. If the franchiser requires franchisees to purchase its products and supplies and does not permit them to buy on the open market, they may pay uncompetitive prices.

IF THE FRANCHISE IS A RESALE

Handling franchise resales is like handling any other business sale, except that it requires some additional steps. The buyer must get the approval of the franchiser. In most cases, the buyer will be asked to submit a financial statement and a plan for the business. Provisions will have to be made for training. The buyer will have to become familiar with and accept all the terms and conditions of the franchise agreement and the requirements that it places on operating procedures. The buyer may have to be interviewed as a part of the franchiser's acceptance procedure.

While these may seem to be added burdens, there is one step that is only possible when handling the sale of a franchise: You and the buyer have the ability to talk to the owners of similar businesses. Talking with other franchisees can give you information and insights unavailable to you with other businesses. You can hear firsthand the experiences of people who own, manage, and work a business very similar to the one you are trying to sell.

IF THE FRANCHISE IS A NEW LOCATION

Only the franchiser or registered representative of the franchiser may sell new or initial franchises. This requirement is imposed as a consumer protection measure. The franchiser must follow very specific steps and must always be accountable for the conduct of the initial sale.

Some business brokerage firms have gone to the considerable trouble to become registered for the sale of initial locations of some franchises. A more practical form of involvement for those who want to include initial franchises as offerings to buyers is to act as a referral agent or finder. Franchise Brokers' Network of Wilmington, Delaware* has developed formal referral relationships with over 60 different franchisers. Franchise Brokers' Network does not sell these franchises; instead, it attracts and qualifies potential buyers and places them in direct contact with officials of the franchise.

HOW YOUR JOB DIFFERS IF THE BUSINESS IS A FRANCHISE

There are several major differences between selling an ongoing business and selling a franchise. We will use the material already discussed in this book to examine some of these differences.

---

*Franchise Brokers' Network
3617A Silverside Road
Wilmington, DE 19810

QUALIFYING BUYERS PERSONALLY

In helping buyers decide what they want (Chapter 6), there are some new choices to be made if they are considering franchises. There is the choice between existing and new franchises, but within all franchises there are other choices. If a buyer is considering a fast-food business, for example, there are franchises featuring pizza, hamburger, and all kinds of sandwiches. Even if the buyer has narrowed the choice to a specific kind of business, like quick printing, there are several franchises from which to choose.

QUALIFYING BUYERS FINANCIALLY

Determining what buyers can afford (Chapter 7) requires a new approach because you do not have historical financial data to analyze and you don't have to go through the complications of pricing the business. The complication you do face is the require-ment to deal with projections of future financial performance. No reputable franchiser will guarantee what the results will be. The buyer will be forced to make judgments and take risks on his or her own evaluation of the franchise and the location.

Of course, you do have a unique source of help that was mentioned earlier, and that is the owners of other franchise locations. You can ask the other owners how close to projection they came. You can learn about the problems and any surprises these owners encountered. You can also ask about any flexibility the franchiser might have with regard to price and terms.

FINDING THE BUSINESS

Finding the business is actually a little easier with a franchise. If you know which one the buyer wants, you can make contact directly. If you don't know, you have all the sources presented in Chapter 4 plus some new ones, such as:

Franchise Opportunities Handbook
Superintendent of Documents
US Government Printing Office
Washington, DC 20402

Membership Directory (and other publications)
International Franchise Association
Suite 1005
1025 Connecticut Ave., NW
Washington, DC 20036

Directory of Franchising Organizations
Pilot Books
347 Fifth Avenue
New York, NY 10016

ANALYZING THE BUSINESS

Analyzing the business (Chapter 9) is the step that will be the most different when the business is a franchise. The whole process of learning about the seller and finding out what he or she wants is not relevant to the purchase of a franchise, where the seller is a company and where the law requires certain disclosures.

The Disclosure Document

Franchisers are required to publish a disclosure document that will give you and the buyer more information than you can ever hope to get from a business owner. It covers:

- The description of the franchise

- The franchiser's ownership and financial condition

- Background data on key people

- The price, royalties, territory, and other terms of the franchise license (including any financing that may be available)

- The operational duties of the franchisee

- Any other obligations of the franchiser, such as training, advertising, and promotion

- The procedures for sale, repurchase, default, termination, renewal, and transfer of the franchise

- The procedure to establish the physical location

- Any litigation in which the franchiser is or has been involved

- Any restrictions on purchases or sales by the franchisee

- Information about past, present, and projected franchise locations, including, where appropriate, the names of the franchisees

Other Franchisees

It is the last item on this list that can help you locate other franchisees. You can get valuable insights into the franchiser's behavior and performance by talking with people who have had firsthand experience. You can find out if promises were kept and how the quality of the goods, services, training, and other support compared to what was expected. If you can locate the former owners of failed locations, you may be able to get some very useful, although possibly tainted, insights into the downside risks of the franchise.

The Franchiser

Of course, the franchiser itself is the prime source of information. You and the buyer may be subjected to a high-pressure sales approach, or you may have to initiate the contact, but either way, there is plenty of information available. The franchiser will want information about the buyer, too. References, a summary of experience, and a financial statement are a minimum. The buyer may also be asked to prepare a business plan to demonstrate his or her ability to manage the franchise.

Judgment Required

The real job in buying a franchise is to exercise good judgment in evaluating the available information:

- *Is the franchise a good value?* What do buyers get that they couldn't provide for themselves or obtain by buying a nonfranchise for the same price?
- *Is the franchiser reputable and financially stable?* Are the people competent and trustworthy?
- *Do you have confidence that the financial projections you have developed are realistic and achievable?* The key element in the projections is the market potential.
- *Does this franchise satisfy the buyer's basic criteria, and does it meet the risk preferences established in Chapter 6?* Will the buyer like it, and can the buyer run it?

11

Negotiations and the Closing

The final sequence of events involves:

- The offer—possibly followed by a series of counter offers
- An accepted offer—usually with some contingencies
- The due diligence examination—and the satisfaction of the contingencies
- The drawing of the formal contract
- The closing

You will negotiate each of these steps, sometimes directly with the buyer and seller, sometimes through their advisors. Worksheet 12 can help you stay organized.

THE NEGOTIATIONS

Negotiating is the process whereby two parties who need or want something from each other find a way to reach an agreement. The solution can be obtained through force, through compromise, through concessions, or some combination of these methods.

As an example, consider a buyer and seller who are far apart on the price of a business. If the seller has made a commitment to move out of the area in a short time and the buyer knows it, the buyer can exert economic force (called the "take-it-or-leave-it" technique). If the seller has no such deadline, he or she may work out a compromise price with the buyer (known as "splitting the difference"). Or the buyer might agree to make a concession on the offered price if the seller will concede good terms of sale (an example of "this for that").

Effective negotiation has some natural enemies: fear, surprise, futility, and suspicion. The best defenses are facts, consistency, alternatives, and honesty. Being honest does not mean being naive or revealing how strongly the buyer may want the business. It does mean that the buyer honestly wants to buy the business but can honestly walk away from it. Although there is no requirement for openness and candor, deception can be detrimental to negotiations.

The discussion of negotiations that follows is based on six Ps: Perspective, Preparation, Posture, Proposal, Persuasion, and Preservation.

PERSPECTIVE

Perspective is needed to insure that the negotiations stay within the bounds of personal values and your client's financial objectives. One way to gain perspective is to understand that people act in their own *perceived* best interest. It doesn't matter that something may actually not be in a person's best interest; the important thing is how it is perceived. A person's perception of reality is, after all, that person's reality.

A good way to maintain your perspective is to remain aware that the buyer does not have to buy the business and the seller does not have to sell. Now that you know how to find businesses and buyers, you can turn up other candidates. This doesn't mean you shouldn't be fully committed to working for the completion of the purchase. It does mean you should not pursue the deal "at any cost."

Your perspective should embrace the following facts about the business buying negotiations:

- The buyer doesn't have to buy the business.
- The seller may not have to sell, at least not to this buyer.
- Negotiations will take longer than expected.

- There will be misunderstandings, and things will go wrong.
- You may learn things during the negotiations that will change your position on some points.

PREPARATION

Preparation for negotiations involves learning as much as you can about the seller, the business, and the buyer. One fact has more impact on the negotiations than any other and cannot be emphasized enough—*you must find out what the seller wants*.

This is not as easy as it sounds. The seller may say one thing and mean another. The seller may not know what he or she wants. The seller may want things that appear irrational. You need to probe any answer you are given to learn what reasons the seller has for wanting something. You may uncover what the seller really wants in the process.

A typical example involves a seller who claims to want all-cash terms. If you probe for the reasons, you might hear "I want to retire, and therefore I need all cash." The seller might be better off with a steady income from the higher price and extended interest-bearing terms the buyer plans to offer. Another common reason given is "I just want to walk away from the business with no worries, therefore I want all cash." Extending terms shouldn't have to mean any worries for the seller. Buyers can provide excellent collateral. Perhaps the seller has worries about the business not being as sound as it's been represented.

The seller may want many things in some amount, and some of these items may be contradictory:

- A high price
- All cash at closing
- Solid security
- Freedom from work
- Freedom from worry
- A reputation for getting a certain (high) price for the business
- Recognition
- A feeling of "winning"
- A stream of income/an annuity

- A quick deal
- A payment method to reward "potential"
- A continuing association
- Status
- A place to go/something to do
- Another business
- To get out from under this business
- Continued employment for friends or relatives
- Relief from debt
- Inclusion or exclusion of real estate
- To please a family member
- To buy or pay for something

The list is not complete, but it illustrates how complex the issue can be.

The reason it's so important to know the seller's wants is that they determine what structure the seller will find most acceptable. Knowing what the seller truly wants can permit you to develop creative alternatives.

An example is a seller who wants to retain ownership of the business real estate. The buyer wants the real estate and is prepared to pay full appraised value. By probing, the buyer finds out that the seller wants to keep the real estate to be able to have rental income. You then develop a creative alternative by finding some other income-producing property for the seller to purchase. The seller buys the other property and gets the rental income, and the buyer gets the business real estate.

Other preparation will involve keeping all advisors well informed and ready to support their clients' efforts. Prepare alternative courses of action by presupposing what will happen. (If A happens, you will do one thing, but if B happens, you will do another.)

POSTURE

Posture has to do with opening positions; that is, how the negotiations will be conducted (such as directly or through intermediaries), where any meetings will be held, and the tone and pace of the negotiations.

A good, clear posture helps to prevent surprises. Abrupt changes in the flow of negotiations can put the parties off balance. Although that tactic may earn some temporary advantage, it most often raises the other party's defenses against any future surprises.

Parties to negotiations sometimes adopt artificial postures to gain a negotiating advantage. Sellers may try to appear uninterested in selling or may give the impression that several offers are pending. Buyers sometimes offer an extremely low price and then permit themselves to be brought up slowly as they gain other concessions. Other buyers offer a very high price that encourages the seller to make generous concessions and then reduce their offer as they find "problems."

Unless you are a very skilled negotiator or unless special circumstances exist, adopt a posture that is comfortable for you to maintain. To the extent you can, be cordial, polite, and businesslike. Be firm but patient. Be open for ideas and alert for opportunities to built toward a successful resolution. Recognize any "gamesmanship" for what it is and attempt to move the negotiations to a higher tone. Don't be rushed and don't be pressured. Review your agency responsibilities with both parties. Once you have developed your perspective, done your preparation, and decided on your negotiating posture, you are ready to put together a proposed offer.

THE PROPOSAL

The centerpiece for the negotiations from this point on is the written proposed offer. It should contain at least these elements:

- A description of what the buyer is offering to purchase and the name(s) of the seller(s)
- The date of the offer and the date the offer expires
- The price
- The terms
- The interest rate, if any
- The repayment schedule, if any
- The amount of deposit, if any
- A date for closing
- The contingencies attached to the offer

A sample "Offer to Purchase" form is presented as Appendix G at the back of this book.

CONTINGENCIES

There are two kinds of *contingencies*. One kind makes the offer subject to the occurrence of some activities. For example, the offer may be contingent upon an examination of the books and records or the assignment of the lease. The second kind of contingency makes the offer subject to the existence of certain conditions. For example, the offer may be contingent upon the level of inventory or the value of certain assets.

Contingencies are put into an offer to break a typical log jam in negotiations. On one hand, the buyer can't make an intelligent offer without facts about the business. On the other, the seller doesn't want to open up the confidential details about the business to someone who may not buy it.

The solution that has developed is the contingent offer. The seller provides information to the buyer but does not allow the buyer to review the books, talk to employees, or the like. The seller provides only enough information to enable the buyer to make a decision and develop an offer. The buyer submits an offer based on the information provided by the seller but reserves the right to withdraw the offer, cancel any agreements, and have the deposit returned if, upon examination by the buyer, the information is not correct or certain conditions are not met. This examination is called *due diligence*.

The wording of the contingent conditions is very important. Buyers prefer that the contingencies be as broad as possible so that any decision to buy or not buy is within their control. An example of a broad contingency is "all financial data is subject to examination and approval by the buyer's accountant." The practical impact of this statement is to give the buyer complete access to the financial records with no obligation to complete the deal. The accountant just has to "disapprove" the financial data. Sellers want the contingencies very narrow so that they are clearly identifiable and easy to meet. A narrow contingency would be "this offer is subject only to the buyer's verification that sales, costs, and expenses were as shown on the financial statements given to the buyer."

The contingencies should cover anything critical to the decision. Verification of financial data is almost always needed. If certain employees or customers are essential, the contingencies can include satisfactory agreements with them. The same applies to contracts with key suppliers or the franchiser, if there is one.

The most common contingency involves the future rent or purchase of the business location. If the decision to buy the business is based on assuming the present lease or renegotiating other arrangements, the buyer will establish such a contingency in the offer (see Figure 11–1). If the buyer is going to borrow money to buy the

---

If you are helping to negotiate a real-estate lease, take the time to understand this important transaction. Above all, if the transaction calls for taking over the seller's lease, review it personally with the parties' attorneys early in the negotiations.

There are several reasons for reviewing the lease in detail as soon as possible:

- Sellers don't always remember the terms and conditions or the revisions to them.
- The seller may have changed the use of the premises or the hours of operation to something not allowed. The landlord may not be aware of it.
- The lease, its assignability, or its renewability, may be legally flawed.
- While the lease may appear assignable, it is still usually subject to the landlord's approval. While the lease may say that the landlord may "not unreasonably withhold approval," landlords sometimes try to extract higher rent by threatening to withhold or delay approval.
- The terms of responsibility for taxes, maintenance, and insurance need to be understood. The difference between a rate quoted "gross" (the three items are included) or quoted "triple net" (the three items are paid additionally by the tenant) can be significant.
- Whether you are negotiating a new lease or assuming an existing one, do not be intimidated by the rigid boilerplate language in a standardized lease form. You should negotiate for the best terms and conditions you can obtain.
- Lease negotiations involve attorneys and take time to complete.

The lease that you help negotiate may make the difference between a viable business transaction and one that cannot be completed.

Figure 11–1. Negotiating the Lease

business, he or she might want to make the offer subject to the ability to obtain financing. Buyers will word their contingencies so that they have the right but not the obligation to withdraw the offer. That is because sometimes, even when contingencies have not been met, they still may want to go forward.

The offer, with all its terms and contingencies, is both critical and complex enough to warrant review by the advisors for both parties.

PERSUASION

Persuasion is convincing another person to accept or do something. Since, as was said earlier, people will only do things that they perceive to be in their own best interest, you must point out to the seller what you believe *is* in his or her best interest and what is not.

An opening negotiating dialogue between you and the seller can be a factual review of the buyer's offer and the reasons for it. Convince the seller to invest time in understanding the offer. It's a way to get the seller participating in reaching a solution.

Learn From Rejection

Be ready to have almost any opening offer rejected and learn all you can from the experience. Do not argue any position yet. Just present the offer and make sure it is understood. Then wring every bit of intelligence you can from the rejection. Keep asking "Why" so that you can understand what is behind the objections. At some point, ask for a counteroffer. Once you have a counteroffer, you can develop more specific negotiating tactics.

Use Concessions

Assess where the parties are far apart and where they are near agreement. Develop a list of concessions the buyer can make and a list of concessions the seller can make. This of as many alternatives as possible to give the parties what they want. Restructure a new offer that reflects the sum of your understanding. This time, you do argue the points.

Price: The Common Stumbling Block

Because price is the most common area of difference, it will be used as an example. The seller may view the price of the business as a reflection of his or her worth. It's common for owners to think of their business as an extension of themselves. They will say, "All those years of hard work should be worth at least this much." You may have to point out that all those years of hard work provided a fine living, a nice home, and so on. The selling price of the business is only the *residual value* of the seller's work. Sellers sometimes base their price on cash taken from the business but never shown on the books. (An admission of tax evasion is not a particularly good testimonial to the seller's honesty.) Whether the cash ever really existed or not, buyers won't accept any pricing logic that cannot be proven.

If the seller does have a genuine logic for the price, find out what it is. Be sure you understand it, and let the seller know that you do. Then you can ask the seller to understand your pricing logic. If you based the price primarily on the value of the assets, ask the seller to explain why it should be higher. If you used a capitalization rate on the cash flow as your pricing method, explain your method to the seller and ask how you can be more accurate.

You may want to compare the seller's price to the cost of duplicating the business. Review with the seller what the cost would be to start a similar business. Let the seller find any flaws in your logic. You might say, "Help me understand why your price is correct when it would cost so much less to start a similar business." Explain that this information will help you convince the buyer.

Keep Your Argument Centered

Your persuasion should always return to the central proposition that the offer is in the seller's best interest. A simple technique is to point out that the buyer wants to pay a fair price and one that will allow him or her to afford to buy the business. Your objective—to see that the buyer is able to buy the business at a fair, affordable price—is in the seller's best interest because it facilitates the sale. Center your argument with the buyer, too. The seller has now provided you with responses to the objections about price. Explain to the buyer that the price allows the seller to achieve his or her objectives and therefore facilitates the sale.

Be Ready for the Worst

Unfortunately, negotiations don't always flow along as logically as in the example. Outbursts of temper, seller regret, ego needs, ill-conceived positions, and almost any other vagary of human nature can turn the negotiations into an emotionally charged circus. A competent intermediary can buffer these frictions and defuse problems before they get out of hand. Your strategy when confronted with an emotional situation should be to acknowledge the other person's strong feelings and begin at once to focus away from personalities and motives and toward a range of solutions.

No detailed script can be written to cover all the variations you will encounter. Use your list of concessions from both sides to persuade the buyer and seller to move toward agreement. Use your advisors as sounding boards and sources of creative strategies and tactics.

PRESERVATION

Preservation of your negotiations involves building upon agreements and narrowing areas of disagreement. It means keeping the negotiations progressing through the stresses and strains that are bound to occur. It means preventing every difference from threatening the whole negotiation and causing it to fall apart.

Poor negotiators and those who rely on power techniques often refer to a particular issue as a "deal breaker." What they mean is that the issue is important. Their overly dramatic reference is intended to put pressure on the other party. The result all too often is to put the negotiations in jeopardy, where any issue can become a deal breaker and no foundation for progress can be built. There may be a time for the dramatic, but negotiations that progress on solid gains stand a much better chance of success. There are several books listed in Resources Literature section at the back of this book that can give you a thorough grounding in negotiation.

THE CLOSING

When negotiations are successful and an agreement is reached, a process for closing the transaction is set up. A formal contract containing all the points of the agreement needs to be drawn up. The seller's attorney usually prepares the first version for review by the buyer and his or her attorney. If the buyer has not yet done his or her due diligence examination, now is the time.

DUE DILIGENCE

The term *due diligence* properly infers an obligation on the buyer's part to satisfy himself or herself regarding the facts of the business. The seller allows the buyer to examine records, books, facilities, and contracts and, if the offer contains such contingencies, to talk with employees, customers, suppliers, and others. The objective is to determine if the information the buyer relied upon in deciding to buy the business is correct. If the offer is typical, it provides the buyer with a way to cancel the agreement if certain information turns out to be untrue. The buyer should use his or her own advisors and the analytical techniques provided earlier. The due diligence examination may result in the withdrawal or revision of the buyer's offer.

Once the contingencies are satisfied and the contract is in its final form, you can lead the transactions to a close. The *closing* is the formal transfer of the business or its assets to the buyer. Unlike a real estate closing, where the routines are well known and are commonly, if not always smoothly, executed, business closings are seldom routine. Each business and the terms of its sale are unique. Even the advisors may not be thoroughly familiar with the intricacies of a business sale. The best way to insure a smooth closing is to compile a checklist. Things may still go wrong, but you will have a blueprint to follow. Where it's appropriate, each item on the checklist should be assigned to someone. More than one closing has been put off because no one brought a copy of the lease.

THE CHECKLIST

The accepted offer agreement reached between the buyer and the seller spelled out the key points of the arrangement. As the formal contracts get hammered out, more and more details are covered. Some of the items in the checklist that follows belong in the contract; others are just reminders of things that need to be done. See Figure 11–2 for a suggested checklist.

The Twilight Time

The first item on the checklist covers what will happen during the time between contract signing and the closing. This time period may last for weeks or months. The buyer might be waiting for financing,

- Conduct of the business until closing
- The time and place of closing
- A list of everyone who needs to attend
- A list of all the documents required
- A breakdown of the funds to be disbursed
- Absolute assurance that the funds are available in the amount and form specified
- New corporate tax and employer identification numbers
- Provision for any licenses to be obtained or transferred
- Prorationing calculations for taxes, wages, utility bills, etc.
- Adjustments for any deposits the seller may have with the landlord, suppliers, or utilities
- Transfer of banking arrangements
- Transfer of keys and alarm codes
- Transfer of any computer codes
- The real estate lease or purchase agreement
- Customer lists
- Transfer of utilities—particularly telephone number
- Any separate contracts establishing seller's obligations to consult or to not compete
- Allocation of the selling price to assets, consulting, noncompete agreement, and goodwill
- Provision for broker's fees
- Clearance of outstanding liens or encumbrances
- Compliance with bulk sales laws to notify suppliers
- Assumption or discharge of any other leases or mortgages
- Definition of the warranties and guarantees the seller will provide
- Provision for security by the buyer
- Definition of the seller's obligations to help in the transition of the business and training of the buyer
- Adjustments for actual inventory and receivables value at closing
- Adjustments in the event that accounts receivable are not collected
- Disposition of any outstanding claims or litigation against or by the seller
- Provision for continuity of insurance or bonding

Figure 11–2. The Closing Checklist

or the seller may be waiting for an up-to-date appraisal. Whatever the reason, provisions have to be made for how the business is to be conducted during that time. Typically, the seller agrees to operate the business in its customary way. The buyer may want to spell out specific dos and don'ts, especially as they relate to *prices*—a big discount price sale can bring in quick money, deplete inventory, and load up customers; *purchasing*—failing to buy needed goods and supplies can conserve the seller's cash but leave the buyer in a bad opening position; and *people*—hiring and firing at this stage can create real problems for a buyer just as he or she is learning the new business.

Asset Sale Versus Stock Sale

Another important item on the checklist is deciding on the method of sale. In most cases, the sale method will be a *sale of assets*. The assets are identified, and the title is passed, usually with some warranties, such as the collectability of the accounts receivable and the quality of the inventory. If liabilities are to be assumed, they are carefully defined.

The alternative method is a *stock sale*, where the buyer purchases the shares of stock of a business. Under some conditions, there are advantages to a stock sale. If the company has tax losses to carry forward, a favorable lease, or other important contracts, or if the assets of the business are encumbered, a stock sale may be the best method to use. The big risk with purchasing the stock of a corporation is that the buyer is also purchasing all liabilities, both known *and unknown*. A lawsuit over some past activity by the company could prove to be a most unwelcome and expensive surprise. If the stock sale method seems worth using, the buyer can attempt to get the seller to indemnify the buyer for any claims that may be made. The importance of these actions and the changing legal and tax environment make having expert advice essential throughout this phase.

Manage Your Closing

The purpose of the checklist is to insure that, after all your hard work to bring buyer and seller together, some glitch doesn't develop at the last minute. A tantrum at the closing table over some mistake or omission is the last thing you want now. Unfortunately, it happens all too often because people underestimate the complexity of the transaction. How you manage the closing can be the single most important part of the transaction.

WORSHEET 12

Negotiation Data Sheet

A. **People**

	Name/Address	Telephone Business	Home
Seller			
Seller's attorney			
Seller's accountant			
Your attorney			
Your accountant			
Broker			
Other			
Other			
Other			

B. **What the Seller Wants Most**

1. _____   2. _____   3. _____

C. **Opening Positions**

	Seller	Buyer
Price		
Cash down payment		
Terms:		
Years		
Interest rate		
Other		
Other		

D. **Possible Concessions**

Seller could concede:
1. _____
2. _____
3. _____
4. _____
5. _____

Buyer could concede:
1. _____
2. _____
3. _____
4. _____
5. _____

After the Closing

During the long hard process of listing and selling the business, the buyer has probably come to respect your opinion and value your advice. If there are specific problems and needs you will, of course, help out where you can. Very often, though, the buyer's first question is a much more general, "What do I do now?" Here is some advice offered to new business owners in *How to Leave Your Job and Buy a Business of Your Own*.* You may wish to pass it along to your buyer.

BE CAUTIOUS ABOUT MAKING BIG CHANGES

The new owner's objective in the early days of ownership is to take control of the new business. It's a time to immerse himself or herself and learn.

The new owner can't know all the critical interdependencies in the business yet, and should be careful about making sweeping or dramatic changes. Changing the name of the business might mean losing old customers. In changing from one supplier to another, the owner may discover that that supplier's brother is (or was) his or her biggest customer. If the business is on a fairly even keel, change should occur slowly.

---

*C. D. Peterson, *How to Leave Your Job and Buy a Business of Your Own* (New York: McGraw-Hill, 1988).

PUT OUT FIRES

Of course, where there are serious problems, the owner must take some action. If the crisis involves relationships with other people— such as customers, employees, or creditors—a new owner can often buy time by listening to the issue, acknowledging the concern, and demonstrating a sincere intent to resolve the problem. Most reasonable people will give a new owner time to learn the facts and come back with a proposed solution.

No matter what the crisis, help is near. Everyone around him or her has a stake in the new owner's success, including the former owner. The former owner will have a special interest in the success of the business when the new owner owes him or her money. There may be a case when the new owner will have to decide alone, but that's why he or she wanted to own a business.

LEARN THE ROUTINES AND THE CULTURE

Every business has its own flow and rhythms. Even when change seems necessary, it's important to learn the culture. The small secrets contained in everyday actions may be the keys to success or the barriers to progress.

FOCUS ON PEOPLE

The new owner's first days should be full of people contact. No matter how trite it sounds, people are what business is mostly about. Human skills, needs, and resources form the basis for production of any kind. These people can provide valuable information on key opportunities for and threats to the business.

EMPLOYEES

The new owner needs to get to know his or her people, their skills and knowledge. He or she should determine if they are satisfied or not and why and should set up a communications pattern that can be sustained. Harm can be done by starting a program of heavy communication and then withdrawing. As important as listening is, it's also important for the new owner to talk to employees. They will want to get to know him or her as an important person in their lives, and they will want to know what the owner plans to do because it affects them very much. To the extent that he or she can, the new owner should offer reassurance that nothing harmful to them is imminent.

CUSTOMERS

How successful the new owner is at communicating with customers may very well determine how successful the business will be. The new owner now controls what the company does and has the power to satisfy his or her customers. Listening to their needs and comments is a top-priority activity, as is finding a way to build an ongoing dialogue.

SUPPLIERS

New owners sometimes overlook these important people, even though, to one extent or another, they rely on them. Because the success of the suppliers already depends on the success of the new business, they should be a part of the business team.

BANKERS, LENDERS, AND INVESTORS

A big fear many new business owners have is that their banker or investor will try to interfere with the business. To try to prevent this intrusion, new owners sometimes do the worst thing possible—they try to keep these people out of the business and in the dark. The new owner's best course of action is finding out what the lenders and investors expect from him or her and trying to give it to them. If they are kept informed about performance, they will usually stay out of the way. If the business does get into trouble, they will want to help.

ADVISORS

Good working relationships with advisors is essential. The new owner's accountant is a critically important person. Sometimes new owners also find that they need some specialized advice from consultants or others. Seminars and books are available on topics ranging from personnel hiring and training to advertising to negotiating with vendors. No matter what kind of advice a new owner needs, the chances are that someone is out there offering it for sale.

SET SIMPLE CONTROLS

At the early stages of ownership, the new owner needs to decide which few critical factors could cause major damage or possible failure for the business. Once these have been identified, controls can be established. Controls may be needed on cash, quality, expenses, purchasing, or some area of employee performance, for example. In the beginning, the new owner should pick only the most important factors and try to keep the controls easy to administer. For example, he or she could require that all purchases or expenditures over a certain amount have his or her approval. The new owner probably will want to personally approve all hiring decisions and perform his or her own quality control spotchecks.

LEARN HOW TO MEASURE RESULTS

The new owner may be surprised at how results are really measured in smaller companies. While financial results are the final measure, they are incomplete, and the reports are available only long after they can do much good. The true indicators of results may be the number of telephone calls per day or the labor hours per unit or the number of days' backlog in the order book. Every business has measures of productivity that will predict results. He or she will need to find out what they are in the new business and begin tracking the business's progress.

DEFINE KEY OPPORTUNITIES AND THREATS

Whether or not the new owner actively develops a formal business plan will depend on his or her philosophy about planning and the requirements of lenders and investors. Regardless of what he or she thinks of business plans, it is important to at least define the key opportunities and threats the business faces. The new owner should review this subject in discussions with employees, customers, and others, and if the business is part of an association, get its views. The local Chamber of Commerce and neighboring businesses are two other good sources of ideas.

The buyer is about to take the steps that will lead to your owning your own business, with all the rewards and responsibilities that go with it. You will be the one who will have to bring everything together. You will have to find, analyze, negotiate, finance, and buy the business. Once that has been accomplished, you will learn the lesson that all new business owners learn—nothing happens unless *you* make it happen.

> Now that you have finished this book we hope you are encouraged to add business opportunity sales to your repertoire of skills. This specialty can provide income, security, and the great satisfaction of helping sellers get full value for their long efforts and helping buyers achieve their dreams.

Exclusive Listing Agreement

EXCLUSIVE LISTING AGREEMENT

This Exclusive Listing Agreement is made as of the date of execution by and between **C.D. PETERSON ASSOCIATES, INC.**, hereinafter referred to as Broker, and _____

authorized to sell the business described below, hereinafter referred to as Seller.

Type of Business _____ Incorporated _____ Yes _____ No

dba _____

Established _____ Years   Financial Year Ends _____ Day _____ Mo.   Present Owner _____ Years

Days of Operation _____ Hours of Operation _____

License Required _____

Furniture, Fixtures & Equipment: $ _____   Inventory at Cost: _____ Included

Annual Gross Sales $ _____ (approx.)   Annual Owner Income $ _____ (approx.)

Bldg. Size _____ Sq. Ft.   Lease Exp. Date _____

Base Monthly Rent $ _____   Lease Renewal Otion _____ yrs.

Landlord _____   Phone # _____

Parking _____ (approx.)   Utility Cost $ _____

1.   Seller hereby authorizes and grants to Broker the sole and exclusive right and authority to list and to

find a purchaser of the business

known as _____

located at _____ on the

following price, terms and conditions or at such other price, terms and condition as shall be acceptable to Seller:

A.   Type of Sale _____   Corp. Stock Sale _____   Asset Sale _____

B.   Items Not Included in Sale _____

_____

_____

Price $ _____   Down Payment $ _____

D.   Terms _____

_____

222

E. Other Conditions of Sale

2. Seller agrees that the assets set forth on the addendum if attached hereto shall be included in the sale.

3. Seller warrants the accuracy of the information furnished herewith or from time to time hereafter with respect to the above described business and agrees to hold the Broker, all such cooperating brokers, and all agents, employees, officers, directors, shareholders and affiliates of Broker or such cooperating brokers harmless from any liabilities or damages arising out of incorrect or undisclosed information, and in addition, Seller shall reimburse Broker and each such person for any costs, including reasonable attorney's fees arising out of any such loss, claim, damage or liability.

4. Seller hereby grants this exclusive right and authority to Broker for a minimum period of _____ months from the date of this Agreement.

5. Seller agrees to provide to the Broker financial statements for the years _____ _____ within ten days of the date of this Agreement.

6. Broker agrees to use reasonable effort to find a purchaser for said business on said price, terms and conditions.

7. Seller agrees to pay Broker as compensation for services rendered a fee of _____ percent of the selling price, but no less than the sum of $_____, upon Broker's procuring a purchaser during the term hereof on the price, terms and conditions specified herein or on any other price, terms and conditions acceptable to Seller, said compensation to be paid at closing of sale.

8. Seller agrees that all purchase offer deposit funds will be retained in a Trustee account of **C.D. Peterson Associates, Inc.**, until final closing of the sale.

In any case of forfeiture of any deposit or down payment funds, the deposit or downpayment funds shall be divided equally between the Seller and Broker.

9. If the business is sold, exchanged, or otherwise transferred: a) during the term hereof by Seller, or through any other source except Broker or any cooperating Broker authorized by Broker to find a Purchaser for said business, or b) within twelve (12) months after the termination of this Agreement to persons with whom Broker, any such cooperating broker, Seller or any such other source shall have negotiated during the term hereof, then the above compensation shall immediately be due and payable to the Broker.

10. As used herein, the term "sale" is defined as any transfer, conveyance, merger, consolidation, exchange or disposition of the business by Seller, including, without limitation, the sale, consignment assignment, lease or hypothecation of the business or its capital, capital stock or assets or any portion of said business, capital, capital stock or assets.

11. As used herein, the term "sales price" shall mean any and all amounts of money or other consideration paid or conveyed to Seller or for its benefit or paid or conveyed by a purchaser in connection with the sale of the business, including, without limitation, cash, inventory, stock, bonds, indenture, debenture, promissory notes, negotiable instruments, royalties, property, letters or lines of credit, loans, bonuses, consulting and employment agreements, non-competition, partnership, rental and lease liabilities, as the case may be, or any combination of the above or other such items of consideration or value.

12. Seller and each signatory hereto on behalf of Seller represents and warrants that Seller and each such signatory hereto is duly authorized to represent all owners, direct or indirect, of the business and to enter into this Agreement, and that all such owners are bound by the terms and conditions of this Agreement.

13. Seller agrees that, if this listing is cancelled or the business withdrawn from sale during the listing term by Seller, the full commission shall become immediately due by Seller to Broker. If Seller refuses or is unable to comply with the listing terms for any reasons, thereby preventing the sale of the business upon the terms and conditions set forth herein, the full commission shall become immediately due by the Seller to the Broker.

14. In the event of the breach of this Agreement by Seller, Seller shall pay to Broker the actual amount of any costs and legal fees incurred by Broker for legal consultation or representation arising therefrom in addition to any other relief which Broker may be entitled to obtain.

15. During the existence of this Agreement, Seller shall refer to Broker all inquiries it may receive or be aware of concerning the sale of the business.

16. Seller hereby acknowledges that he has read this Agreement and has received a copy of it.

17. In consideration of the execution hereof, this Agreement shall be binding upon the Seller, and Seller's successors, heirs and assigns.

Executed this _____ day of _____, 19____

C.D. PETERSON, BROKER

By: _____

SELLER

Print Name _____

By: _____

Title: _____

Address: _____

SELLER

Print Name _____

By: _____

Title: _____

Address: _____

White To File — Canary To Broker — Pink To Client

B

Confidential Receipt of Information Form

C. D. PETERSON ASSOCIATES, INC.
CONFIDENTIAL RECEIPT OF INFORMATION

The undersigned acknowledges receipt of the below described information, materials or other items from C. D. Peterson Associates, Inc., herein referred to as CDPAI.

The undersigned acknowledges and understands that CDPAI is merely transmitting, without warranty, information, data and material supplied by the owner and/or his employees and associates. CDPAI makes no representation as to its accuracy nor has it made any attempt or effort, by independent investigation, to verify any such information, data and material concerning said business. CDPAI shall not be accountable or liable for its accuracy. Further, the undersigned acknowledges and understands that CDPAI makes no warranties or representations concerning the accuracy of such material.

The undersigned further acknowledges that such information and material, as well as the fact of our negotiations are confidential and represents and warrants that same will not be disclosed to any other person or party except the legal and financial advisors of the undersigned who may be furnished such information for the purpose of advising the undersigned as to a proposed purchase of the subject company. The undersigned hereby states that he/she is a potential buyer and is not searching for information for any competitive, governmental, or legal use.

CDPAI declares that the undersigned must, independently, investigate and verify the information supplied by CDPAI as well as to independently undertake a careful and diligent research of all aspects of the said business so that a sound evaluation of it may be made by the undersigned.

The undersigned further agrees that all dealings concerning said business opportunity will be handled through CDPAI.

The undersigned is advised that Seller may be responsible for any fees due CDPAI should a sales transaction take place with the undersigned during the 12 month period following the date of the expiration of the listing agreement.

The undersigned understands that he/she is aware of the sensitivity of these discussions and that they may affect the employees of said business and agrees that they will refrain from initiating any direct or indirect contact without express written approval.

The undersigned further agrees that he/she will not knowingly solicit employment of employees of said business or customers for a period of one year from the time that discussions cease.

At such time as interest in this matter ceases or negotiations are not continued, the undersigned agrees that he/she will promptly return all originals and copies of information furnished and destroy all notes and copies thereof made on this matter.

Business Name: _____

File # _____

Type of Information:

Financials	_____	Write-Up	_____
Proforma	_____	Prospectus	_____
Equipment List	_____	Pictures	_____
Tax Returns	19____ 19____ 19____	Appraisal	_____
Brochure	_____	Other	_____

Name of person receiving information: _____

Address: _____

On behalf of: _____

I have read the above and I hereby acknowledge that CDPAI makes no representation or warranty as to the correctness, completeness or accuracy of any information, data and material supplied by it to me, now and hereafter, concerning the above mentioned business, and that it is my sole responsibility to verify to my satisfaction said information, data and material. I understand that any decision to purchase this business must be based on my own analysis and judgement.

Signature: _____ Date: _____

226

C

Company Profile Data Form

1. General Information

Source of contact

Co. name _____   _____

Address _____   _____

_____   _____

_____   Date _____

Owner's Name _____

Phone _____   _____

Business   Home

Business description _____

_____

_____

_____

_____

How owned: sole proprietor _____ partnership _____ corporation _____ type of corp _____

Reason for selling: _____

Seller will not compete for _____ years and _____ miles.

Seller will train: yes _____ no _____ How long: _____

What are the outstanding features of the business? _____

_____

Special skills or licenses needed: _____

Business hours _____

Current market conditions and outlook _____

2. Price and Terms

Asking price: $ _____ Inventory included: $ _____ Additional: $ _____

Type of sale: Asset _____ Stock _____

Seller desires _____ % of the total selling price as a down payment.

Seller will carry the balance at _____ % interest for _____ years.

Interest only: yes ____ no ____ Balloon payment: yes ____ no ____ After ____ years.

Any equipment leases to be assumed by the buyer? yes _____ no _____

Approximate total lease payments: $ _____ per month for _____ years.

Seller will consider exchange: yes _____ no _____ For _____

(type of property)

Approximate inventory value at cost _____ as of _____ 19 _____

3. People

Owner's duties: _____

_____

_____

Key people

Title	Years Employed and Duties
_____	_____
_____	_____
_____	_____
_____	_____

Total employees excluding seller: _____ full time; _____ part time.

Overall assessment of people: _____ _____

_____

_____

_____

Owner's and key employees' status after sale: _____

_____

_____

_____

_____

4. Equipment, Furniture, Fixtures

Item	Age	Cost If Known	Estimated Value
_____	____	_____	_____
_____	____	_____	_____
_____	____	_____	_____
_____	____	_____	_____
_____	____	_____	_____
_____	____	_____	_____
_____	____	_____	_____
_____	____	_____	_____
_____	____	_____	_____
_____	____	_____	_____

5. Real Estate

Approx. size of lot: _____ sq. ft. acres   property zoned: _____
Approx number of parking spaces: _____
Number of buildings _____ Approx. size of building: _____ sq. ft.
Type of construction (if known): _____
Approx. age of building _____ ; Living quarters: yes _____ no _____
Storage area: yes __ no __ Loading area: yes __ no __ Repairs needed: yes __ no __
Is the real estate for sale? yes _____ no _____ Price $ _____
Is the property for lease? yes _____ no _____ Monthly rent $ _____
Additional override rent (if any): _____
Common area charge (if any): $ _____ Original length of lease: _____
Time left on current lease: _____ Expires (month and year): _____
Lease deposit (if any): $ _____ Lease purchase option: yes _____ no _____
Other options
Is lease assumable? yes _____ no _____

6. Summary of Financials

Income Statement
For the period _____ to _____

Sales		$ _____
Cost of sales	$ _____	
Gross profit		$ _____
Expenses		
Owner's salary		$ _____
Owner's benefits		_____
Employee salaries (no. of people _____)		_____
Employee benefits		_____
Rent		_____
Utilities		_____
Travel and entertainment		_____
Selling expenses		_____
Depreciation		_____
Insurance		_____
Interest		_____
Automobile		_____
Legal and accounting		_____
Other _____		_____
Other _____		_____
Other _____		_____
Total expenses		$ _____
Pretax profit		$ _____

Balance Sheet
as of _____

Current Assets:
    Cash   \$ _____
    Accounts receivable   _____
    Notes receivable   _____
    Inventory   _____
    Prepaid expenses   _____
    Other   _____
Total Current Assets   \$ _____

Fixed Assets:
    Furniture, fixtures, machinery, and equipment   \$ _____
    Less: accumulated depreciation   _____   \$ _____
    Land and buildings   _____
    Less: accumulated depreciation   _____   \$ _____
Total Fixed Assets   \$ _____
Total Assets   \$ _____

Liabilities and Owner's Equity

Current Liabilities: \$ _____
    Accounts payable   _____
    Wages payable   _____
    Taxes payable   _____
    Interest payable   _____
    Notes/leases (current portion)   _____
    Services or products owed to customers   _____
    Other liabilities
Total Current Liabilities   \$ _____

Long-term Liabilities:
    Notes   \$ _____
    Mortgages   _____
    Other _____   _____
Total Long-term Liabilities   \$ _____

Owner's equity:
    Capital stock   \$ _____
    Retained earnings   _____
Total Liabilities and Owner's Equity   \$ _____

7. Evaluation

Rating versus Criteria—Chapter 3 (Use 1-to-10 scale; 10 is best)

Cash flow	_____	Growth potential	_____
Location	_____	Working condition	_____
Liquidity	_____	Status and image	_____
People intensity	_____	Competition	_____
Overall desirability	_____	Content of the business	_____
	Total _____ + 10 = _____ rating		

Risk Evaluation—Chapter 4 (Use 1-to-6 scale: 6 is low risk)

Company history	_____	Special skills required	_____
The industry segment	_____	Special relationships required	_____
Location	_____	Labor situation	_____
Return *of* investment	_____	Management situation	_____
Return *on* investment	_____	Outside dependency	_____
Company reputation	_____	Products/services	_____
Competition	_____	Franchises/Licenses required	_____
Technology	_____	Legal exposure	_____
	Total _____ + 16 = _____ rating		

Contact Follow-Up Record

Date of Contact	With (Name)	Topics Discussed	Date to Follow Up
_____	_____	_____	_____
_____	_____	_____	_____
_____	_____	_____	_____
_____	_____	_____	_____
_____	_____	_____	_____
_____	_____	_____	_____
_____	_____	_____	_____
_____	_____	_____	_____
_____	_____	_____	_____
_____	_____	_____	_____

D

Sample Selling Brochure

Assisting
Business Owners
Potential Buyers
and
Financial Advisors

In the
Sale, Purchase,
and
Evaluation of
Businesses

C.D. Peterson
Associates, inc.

For business owners who want to sell their business

You've worked hard to build your business and now you want to realize its full value. We are committed to helping you get that full value with a minimum of time and wasted effort.

Understanding   CD Peterson Associates will work hard to thoroughly analyze and understand the facts about your business. We believe that the more we know about you and your business, the better we can help.

Evaluation   Nothing is more critical to the sale of your business than the price and nothing is more critical to determine price than a rigorous and complete evaluation. We will evaluate standard measures such as assets, profits and cash flow and the factors unique to your business such as growth, competition, location, customer goodwill, the terms of sale and many others.

Marketing   Any properly priced business will sell eventually. The objective is to sell the business quickly and to someone who will succeed.

CD Peterson Associates will develop a tailored comprehensive marketing plan which will:
• profile and identify potential buyers
• determine the best way to reach them and effectively present your business.

This can involve the use of personal contacts, selective telemarketing, targeted direct mail, brochures and other advertising including newspaper ads.

In addition, we work with and maintain an up to date data file of people actively seeking to buy a business of their own.

The marketing plan will be individually tailored to find qualified potential buyers and to sell your business quickly.

Confidentiality and Support   When confidentiality is important in getting the full value for your business, our organization will provide the type of confidentiality appropriate to the sale.

We will provide you with sound and creative support throughout the negotiations to keep the process moving to a successful closing.

C.D. Peterson
Associates, inc.

For business owners who want to acquire additional businesses

Your business is doing well and you want to grow but acquisitions take time and specialized effort. We can find, screen and negotiate with your acquisition candidates while you manage your business.

Understanding   CD Peterson Associates will spend whatever time is necessary with you and your organization to fully understand the growth objectives and strategies for your business. Understanding your unique needs is basic to developing sound recommendations.

Search Plan   The first key to a successful acquisition is to find the right business. We will develop a search plan that will:
• establish the criteria for the right business
• research and identify candidates
• effectively solicit their interest

The plan will rely primarily on targeted marketing techniques and an expanding network of personal contact activity.

Evaluation   The second key to a successful acquisition is to pay the right price. CD Peterson Associates will evaluate your candidates on both standard financial measures and on other less tangible measures unique to the criteria you established. Special attention will be paid to areas of potential savings or exposure in the future combination of the two businesses.

Confidentiality and Support   If potential sellers know too early who the buyer is, it can influence their price expectations or even their willingness to sell.

In addition not every contact will develop into a real candidate. Our organization will provide the confidentiality necessary to protect your time and your negotiating position.

We will provide you with the support needed throughout the process of identification, search, evaluation, and negotiation of a completed acquisition.

C.D. Peterson
Associates, inc.

For those who want to buy a business

You're a first time buyer ready to step out on your own or an experienced business owner looking for a new opportunity. We can help you organize your efforts and find the business that fits your requirements. Or you can review an extensive list of business we offer for sale.

Understanding A personal decision to buy a business involves complex motives. CD Peterson Associates will carefully review your decision with you in order to understand your objectives and expectations.

Financing Strategy At times people need assistance to systematically analyze their resources and financial capabilities. We will help you develop financing strategies consistent with your resources and your objectives. (It should be noted that sellers often finance a portion of the sale of a business.)

Available Listings We maintain a wide variety of businesses available for sale.
- Manufacturing
- Retail
- Service
- Distribution
- Restaurants

The businesses range in size from small to large. Most have seller financing.

Search Plan If we don't have a business you want in our inventory of listings, we can search for it. A personal search for a business does not have to be confined to reading the classifieds. CD Peterson Associates will develop a search plan that will actively seek out businesses that meet your criteria. Often a business becomes for sale when a gratified buyer expresses interest.

We are prepared to offer the patient support required to help you implement this very important decision.

There is, of course, no fee to buyers for any business already listed with us.

CD Peterson Associates, Inc.

For accountants, attorneys and other financial advisors

Your client needs an evaluation for tax purposes, for a divorce settlement, to prepare the business for sale or for other reasons. We can perform that evaluation confidentially and professionally.

Understanding Your client's needs are in your trust. CD Peterson Associates will work closely with you to fully understand those needs in the context of your client's special situation.

Evaluation While no evaluation is completely objective, credibility is best earned by following a clear and logical process. We use both standard technical means and well accepted market factor analyses to develop a value for your client's business.

Sale or Acquisition Your client's needs may involve selling a part or all of a business or acquiring a business. CD Peterson Associates will provide the assistance your client needs from an individually tailored marketing plan to a targeted search plan.

Other sections of this brochure contain additional information on these services.

Confidentiality and Support Your relationship with your client will be fully respected. Our organization will employ the degree of confidentiality you feel is appropriate and will work with you to determine our proper support role.

For all prospective clients

Whether you want to buy, sell or evaluate a business, we can provide professional and personal help. Here are some facts about CD Peterson Associates.

Large and Small Businesses Whether you want to buy a smaller business, divest a division or product line of a large company or sell a medium sized business CD Peterson Associates will help.

We believe that every transaction, regardless of size, is important and deserves professional treatment.

Data Based Systems There is no substitute for personal understanding, careful planning and aggressive execution. To support these activities CD Peterson Associates makes extensive use of computer data base systems.

We use our systems to build files about businesses for sale, to maintain lists of active buyers and their wants, and to help design individual marketing and search plans.

In addition we have proprietary computer programs to help us in evaluation and pricing a business.

Networking To do the best job for you. CD Peterson Associates can engage the services of specialists from a network of active contacts. These can range from specialized appraisers, to tax and accounting professionals, to financial sources.

Using these network resources insures that you get the type of specialized help that you need.

CD Peterson Associates will work closely with your own financial and legal advisors or recommend professionals to you.

Fees and Commissions Because we are an independent corporation providing services tailored to your needs, we can offer flexibility in how we charge for our services:
- per hour fees, based on the type of assignment
- per project fees, based on a defined task
- commission, when assisting in the sale or purchase of a business
- or combination, where fees may become applicable toward reducing a commission.

All assignments and charges will be confirmed in writing.

Call (203) 748-7119

235

E

Personal Promotion Sheet

Arthur L. Haile
Senior Associate
Associated Properties, Inc.
74 James Street
San Francisco, CA 90763
(415) 555-7111

Background:	Eight years experience in real estate, first with large residential properties, then with commercial/retail. Became active in business opportunities in 1986 and am now specializing in the sale of businesses.
Education and Designations:	B. S. from San Francisco State College, Graduate Realtors Institute (G.R.I.)
Recent Accomplishments:	Leased 15 units (25,000 sq. ft.) in Patriot Square Mall.
	Listed and sold 170,000 sq. ft. Executive Office Tower.
	Sold "Daphne's" Restaurant, A & B Auto, Thompson Manufacturing, and several other Bay Area businesses.
	Sales Person of the Year 1987.
Membership and Associations:	San Francisco Board of Realtors
	International Business Brokers Association
	Institute of Business Appraisers
	Downtown Business Club
	Bay Area Chamber of Commerce
	Rotary
	Treasurer, Industrial League

My background in business opportunities—coupled with my memberships, associations, and knowledge of San Francisco—gives me the experience and contacts to be effective in selling businesses.

General Buyer/Finder Agreement

AGGREEMENT

This agreement is made as of the date of execution by and between C. D. Peterson Associates, Inc. hereinafter referred to as the "Finder" and the "Buyer" known as _____ of _____

As it is mutually understood that Buyer is desirous of being introduced to third-party principals for the purpose of effecting the sale, purchase, or exchange of a business interest with these principals, hereinafter referred to as Sellers, and Finder is engaged to effect such an introduction, then it is agreed as follows:

1. Finder shall use its best efforts to introduce Sellers to Buyer for the purpose of effecting a "Sale," which is defined as any transfer conveyance, merger, financing, consolidation, exchange, or disposition of property or business including, without limitation, the sale, consignment, assignment, lease, or hypothecation of a business, its capital, capital stock, or assets or any portion of a business, capital, capital stock, or assets.

2. The "Buyer" shall include, in addition to that named in the Agreement, any affiliates, associates, relatives, or other individuals or entities who obtain information, through the Buyer or through the Seller on behalf of the Buyer, not otherwise available to them and as a result transact a purchase with the Seller.

3. The "Seller" shall include, in addition to the Seller itself, the stockholders and any other controlling persons, any and all subsidiaries, affiliates, joint venturers, successors, or other companies whether associated in equity or beneficially that are involved in any way in the transaction and shall further include any person who directly receives consideration pursuant to this agreement that is not otherwise covered hereby.

4. As used herein, the terms "purchase price" or "consideration" shall mean any and all amounts of money or other consideration paid or conveyed to Seller or for its benefit or paid or conveyed by Buyer in connection with the sale of a business, including, without limitation, cash; stock; bonds; indenture; debenture; your dentures; their dentures; promissory notes; negotiable instruments; royalties; property; letters or lines of credit; loans; bonuses; consulting and employment agreements; noncompetition, partnership, rental, and lease agreements; capital investments; the assumption or discharge of liabilities, as the case may be; or any combination of the above or other items of consideration or value. The "purchase price" in a stock sale shall include in addition to the stock purchase price, all of the liabilities assumed as if the sale were an asset sale.

5. "In cash" shall mean in U.S. dollars unless otherwise specified plus interest at the current prime rate from closing date to the date of actual delivery if delivery is delayed. Cashiers and certified checks, but not personal checks, shall be considered to be cash.

6. "Closing" shall be defined as the time when any consideration is transferred by or to or from the Company. All related transactions shall be deemed a single closing for calculation of Finder's fee. Finder shall be notified by Seller in advance of any and all closings and shall have the right to be but not the obligation of being present.

7. Buyer agrees to pay Finder, as compensation for services rendered, a fee of:

- 10% of the first $1 million of the fair market value passed, as passed at closing plus

- 5% of the next million dollars of the fair market value of any consideration passed, as passed at closing plus

- 4% of the next million dollars of the fair market value of any consideration passed, as passed at closing plus

- 3% of the next million dollars of the fair market value of any consideration passed, as passed at the closing plus

- 2% of the next million dollars of the fair market value of any consideration passed, as passed at the closing plus

- 1% of the fair market value of any and all additional consideration passed, as passed at closing.

The fee shall be paid in full and in cash at closing to the Finder. The payment of the fee shall be an integral and requisite part of any closing and if unpaid and outstanding, in whole or in part, after any closing shall in addition to being guaranteed by the buyer individually, shall constitute a lien on the assets and property transferred at closing in the hands of the receiver.

8. This agreement shall be in effect until terminated and revoked upon ninety (90) working days prior written notice delivered by Buyer to Finder. Furthermore, the term of this agreement shall be extended and the Finder entitled to a fee as defined herein if introduction of a Seller to Buyer results in a Sale, exchange, or purchase during the term of the Agreement or within a five (5) year period thereafter. Unless herein specified, there are no Sellers excluded from this agreement.

9. Buyer agrees to hold all submittals by Finder of names of Sellers and any accompanying information in confidence, not to be disclosed to third parties external to any negotiations or evaluations necessary for the evaluation of the terms of the sale, purchase, or exchange and to return all documents to Finder if no transaction is closed. Finder agrees to hold all information received from Buyer confidential not to be released except in the performance of this contract.

10. Buyer agrees to keep Finder informed as to the state of any change in economic status or intentions. Finder, in turn, agrees to keep Buyer informed of its efforts on Buyer's behalf.

11. Finder does not assume responsibility for, nor guarantee, accuracy or completeness of information provided by Seller. Buyer shall satisfy himself/herself from his/her own or his/her advisors' inspection of Seller's own books, records, and assets as to all pertinent information desired by Buyer.

12. Buyer and each signatory hereto on behalf of Buyer represent and warrant that Buyer and each signatory hereto is duly authorized to represent all owners, direct or indirect, of the business and to enter into this Agreement, and that all such owners are bound by the terms and conditions of the Agreement.

13. It is agreed that in the event of a dispute between Seller and Finder arising out of or connected with this Agreement, or arising out of any other transaction relating to the earning and/or payment of fees, such dispute shall be submitted to arbitration in accordance with the rules then in effect of the American Arbitration Association, and judgment upon the award rendered may be entered in any Court of competent jurisdiction. The parties hereby waive any appeal of the decision of the arbitrators. Each party may be represented by legal counsel in any such proceeding.

14. This Agreement shall be construed under the laws of the State of Connecticut, and the parties agree to submit to the jurisdiction of the courts in the city of Danbury, State of Connecticut.

15. This Agreement constitutes the entire Agreement of the parties and supersedes and terminates all prior agreements, understandings, or arrangements, whether verbal or written. No modifications of any of the terms hereof shall be valid unless the same shall be in writing and signed by the parties hereto.

16. Delivery of any writings required by this agreement shall be deemed delivered as of the date of deposit in the U.S. mail to the last known address of the other party.

17. This Agreement shall be binding upon the Buyer, and the Buyer's successors, heirs, and assigns.

Executed this _____ day of _____, 19____

C. D. PETERSON ASSOCIATES, INC.   BUYER
36 Mill Plain Road, Suite 405
Danbury, CT 06811

By: _____   By: _____

Signed: _____   Title: _____

_____
As Stockholder/Officer

_____
As Individual

G

Purchase Offer Form

BUSINESS OPPORTUNITY PURCHASE OFFER AND DEPOSIT RECEIPT

RECEIVED FROM _____

OF _____ hereinafter designated

as PURCHASER, the sum of ($ _____) _____ DOLLARS

evidenced by funds payable to C.D. Peterson Associates, Inc. Trustee Account, to be deposited in escrow as deposit on account of the PUR-

CHASE PRICE of ($ _____) _____ DOLLARS

for the business situated in the City of _____ , County of _____ , State of _____

located at _____

known as _____

This offer is made contingent upon the terms and conditions as stated herein. Payment terms are as follows:

_____

_____

_____

_____

Contingencies _____

_____

_____

_____

STOCK INVENTORY. Saleable inventory of a minimum amount of $ _____ is included in the purchase offer price stated herein and will be delivered at the closing of this sale/offer. Purchaser will buy any excess amount of saleable inventory at closing at current cost.

FIXTURES AND EQUIPMENT. A total combined value of current assets (not including inventory) of an amount equal to

$ _____ is included in the purchase offer price stated herein and will be delivered at the

closing of this purchase/sale.

244

BUSINESS OPPORTUNITY PURCHASE OFFER AND DEPOSIT RECEIPT

LEASE.

☐ Purchaser to assume the existing lease. This sale is conditioned upon landlord's consent to assignment of said lease prior to closing.

☐ This sale is conditioned upon Purchaser's ability to negotiate a new lease with landlord prior to _____

DUE DILIGENCE DOCUMENTS. The Seller shall deliver to the Purchaser for his approval the following documents within 5 days of acceptance of this offer. Purchaser shall be deemed to have approved said documents unless written notice to the contrary is delivered to Seller or his/her agent within 10 days of receipt by Purchaser, in which case Purchaser may have his deposit returned and both parties shall be relieved of all obligations hereunder. Seller warrants that all such documents will be true and complete.

☐ Inventory of Personal Property Included in the Purchase Price   ☐ **Current Balance Sheet**
☐ **Schedule of Accounts Receivable**   ☐ **Copy of Lease**
☐ **Income and Expense Statements for the years** _____   ☐ **Other**

Purchaser shall indicate approval of said documents and the satisfaction of all contingencies of this offer within 10 days of acceptance of this offer by increasing the escrow deposit amount to $ _____

All escrow deposit funds will be held in a non-interest bearing trust account by C.D. Peterson Associates, Inc. until closing.

DEFAULT. In the event that Purchaser fails to pay the balance of the purchase price, or to complete the purchase as herein provided, Seller may, subject to any rights of the Broker herein, retain all amounts paid hereunder as damages for the breach of this agreement by Purchaser; provided, however, that Seller may take such action as deemed appropriate to collect such additional damages as may have been actually sustained, and that Purchaser shall have the right to take such action as deemed appropriate to recover such portion of the amounts paid hereunder as may be allowed by law. In the event that Purchaser shall so default, Purchaser agrees to pay to Broker, the commission which Broker may have against Seller as hereinafter provided. The obligation of Purchaser to Broker shall be in addition to any rights which Broker may have against Seller in the event of default. In the event legal action is instituted by any party to this agreement to enforce the terms of this agreement, or arising out of the execution of this agreement or the sale, the prevailing party shall be entitled to receive from the other party a reasonable attorney fee to be determined by the court in which such action is brought.

CLOSING. Purchaser and Seller agree to close this sale/purchase on or before _____ , 19 _____

This offer contains the major elements of the agreement to purchase. Purchaser and Seller agree to enter into a formal contract of purchase/sale within 20 days of acceptance of this offer. Some details and modifications may be made in the formal contract document, but agreement thereto shall not be unreasonably withheld.

TIME. Time is of the essence of this agreement. The term "days" as used herein means calendar days unless otherwise specified.

EXPIRATION. This offer shall expire unless a copy hereof with Seller's written acceptance is delivered to the Purchaser or to his/her Agent on or before _____ ☐ AM ☐ PM. on _____ , 19 _____

ACKNOWLEDGEMENTS. Purchaser acknowledges receipt of a copy of this offer. Purchaser acknowledges that he/she has not received or relied upon statements or representations made by the Broker which are not herein expressed, including any statements or representations regarding the effect of this transaction upon Purchaser's Tax Liability. The Broker recommends that Purchaser and Seller obtain professional counsel on any tax or legal questions relating to this transaction.

By _____

C.D. Peterson Associates, Inc. _____ Broker   DATED _____ TIME _____

_____ Purchaser

_____ Purchaser

ACCEPTANCE

The undersigned Seller accepts the foregoing offer and agrees to sell the herein described business for the price and on the terms and conditions herein specified. The undersigned Seller hereby covenants that he is the owner of the above-mentioned business and property and has the legal right to sell the same.

COMMISSION. Seller hereby agrees to pay to C.D. Peterson Associates, Inc., the Broker in this transaction, in cash from proceeds at close of escrow _____ % of the sale price for services rendered. In the event that Purchaser defaults and fails to complete the sale, the Broker shall be entitled to receive one-half of Purchaser's deposit, but not more than the commission earned, without prejudice to Broker's rights to recover the balance of the commission from Purchaser. The mutual recision of this agreement by Purchaser and Seller shall not relieve said parties of their obligations to Broker hereunder. In the event legal action is instituted to collect this commission, or any portion thereof, Seller agrees to pay the Broker such additional sum as the court may adjudge reasonable for attorney fees. This agreement shall not limit the rights of Broker provided for in any listing or other agreement which may be in effect between Seller and Broker, except that the amount of the commission shall be as specified herein.

The undersigned Seller hereby acknowledges receipt of copy hereof. DATED _____ TIME _____

_____ Seller

_____ Seller

Resource Literature

COMPUTER SOFTWARE

BUSINESS LISTINGS

Deal Base, Business Publications, Inc.

DATABASE (FILES AND RECORDS MANAGEMENT)

dBase III Plus, Ashton-Tate. *Cornerstone*, Infocom, Inc. *DataEase*, Software Solutions. *Alpha/Three*, Alpha Software Corporation.

FINANCIAL ANALYSIS AND PLANNING

Javelin, Javelin Software Corporation. *Money Decision Financial Desk Reference*, Silver Eagle Software Publishing.

SPREADSHEETS

IBM Planning Assistant, IBM Corporation. *Lotus 1-2-3*, Lotus Development Corporation. *Microsoft Multiplan*, Microsoft Corporation. *SuperCalc 4*, Computer Associates.

VALUATION

ValuSoft, ValuSoft Co. *DealMaker*, ValuSoft Co. *LBO Plan II*, Venture Economics. *M + A Plan*, ValuSoft Co.

WORD PROCESSING

Multimate, Ashton-Tate. *Multimate Advantage*, Ashton-Tate. *Wordstar*, Micro-Pro International. *Wordstar 2000*, Micro-Pro International.

BOOKS

EVALUATING AND PRICING THE BUSINESS

Bowlin, Oswald D. *Guide to Financial Analysis*. McGraw-Hill, New York, 1979.

Burke, Frank M. *Valuation and Valuation Planning for Closely Held Businesses*. Prentice Hall, 1972.

Desmond, Glenn M., and Kelley, Richard E. *Business Valuation Handbook*. Valuation Press Inc., Marina del Rey, CA, 1980.

Desmond, Glenn, and Marcello, John. *Handbook of Small Business Valuation Formulas*. Marina del Rey, CA, 1987.

Hayes, Rick S., and C. Richard Baker. *Simplified Accounting for Non-Accountants*. John Wiley, New York, 1980.

Miles, Raymond C. *Basis Business Appraisal*. John Wiley, New York, 1984.

Peterson, Carl D. *How to Leave Your Job and Buy a Business of Your Own*. McGraw-Hill, New York, 1988.

Peterson, Carl D. *How to Sell Your Business*, McGraw-Hill, New York, 1990.

Pratt, Shannon. *Valuing a Business: The Analysis and Appraisal of Closely Held Companies*. Dow Jones-Irwin, Homewood, IL, 1983.

Pratt, Shannon. *Valuing Small Businesses and Professional Practices*. Dow Jones-Irwin, Homewood, IL, 1985.

Reisenger, Steven M. *Valuation of Privately Owned Businesses*. Acquisition Planning Inc., Chicago, 1981.

Sweeney, Allen. *Accounting Fundamentals for Non-Financial Executives*. Amacom, New York, 1972.

Tracy, J. A. *How to Read a Financial Report: Wringing Cash Flow and Other Vital Signs Out of the Numbers*, 2nd ed. John Wiley, New York, 1985.

Tray, Leo. *Almanac of Business and Industrial Ratios*. Prentice-Hall, Englewood Cliffs, NJ, annual.

FINANCING SOURCES

Gladstone, David. *Venture Capital Handbook*. Prentice Hall, Englewood Cliffs, NJ, 1988.

Greve, J. Terrence. *1987 Directory of Financing Sources*. Business Publications, Inc., Homewood, IL, 1985.

Haft, Robert J. *Venture Capital and Small Business Financing*. Clark Boardman, New York, 1984.

Hayes, Stephen R., and John C. Howell. *How to Finance Your Small Business with Government Money: SBA and Other Loans*, 2nd Ed. John Wiley, New York, 1983.

Holtz, Herman. *2001 Sources of Financing for Small Businesses*. Arco Publishing, New York, 1983.

Pratt, Stanley E., and Jane K. Morris, (eds.). *Pratt's Guide to Venture Capital Sources*, 10th ed. Venture Economics, Inc., Oryx Press, Phoenix, 1986.

Richardson, Clinton. *The Venture Magazine Complete Guide to Venture Capital*. NAL Books, New York, 1987.

Robins, Adam E. *Getting Your Banker to Say "Yes": Tactics for the Entrepreneur*. Probus, New York, 1985.

Silver, A. David. *Up Front Financing: The Entrepreneurs Guide*. John Wiley, New York, 1982.

Silver, A. David. *Who's Who In Venture Capital*, 2nd Ed. John Wiley, New York, 1986.

Small Business Financing. Shephard's-McGraw-Hill, New York, 1983.

Weissman, Rudolph L. *Small Business and Venture Capital*. Ayer Co., Salem, NH, 1979.

FINDING BUSINESSES

Catalog of Mailing Lists. F. S. Hoffheimer, Mineola, NY.

Colgate, Craig, Jr., (ed.). *National Trade and Professional Associations of the United States*, 18th ed. Columbia Books, New York, 1983.

Direct Mail List Rates and Data. Standard Rate and Data Service, Skokie, IL.

Duns Marketing Services. Parsippany, NJ.

Etheridge, James M., (ed.). *The Directory of Directories*. Gale Research Co., Detroit, 1985.

Gruber, Katherine, (ed.). *Encyclopedia of Associations*, 20th ed. Gale Research Co., Detroit, 1986.

Lists of 14 Million Businesses Compiled From the Yellow Pages. American Business Lists, Omaha, annual.

The National Business List, Market Data Retrieval. Shelton, CT, quarterly.

Polk Mailing List Catalog. R. L. Polk & Co., Taylor, MI.

Thomas Register of American Manufacturers and Thomas Register Catalog File. Thomas Publishing Co., New York, annual.

U.S. Business Directories: 600 Directories Compiled From Yellow Pages. American business directors, Omaha, annual.

FRANCHISING

Raiffa, Howard. *The Art and Science of Negotiating.* Pilot Books, New York, 1986.

Franchise Annual: Handbook and Directory. Info Press, Lewiston, NY, annual.

Franchise Opportunities Handbook. Office of Consumer Goods and Service Industries, U.S. Dept. of Commerce, U.S. Government Printing Office, Washington, D.C., 20402.

LEGAL

Goldstein, Arnold S. *Business Transfers, An Accountant and Attorney's Guide.* John Wiley, New York, 1986.

Hancock, William A. *The Small Business Legal Advisor.* McGraw-Hill, New York, 1982.

Lane, Mark J. *Legal Handbook for Small Business.* American Management Association, New York, 1978.

Lane, Mark J. *Purchase and Sale of Small Businesses: Tax and Legal Aspects.* John Wiley, New York, 1985.

Stewart, David O. *Representing Small Businesses.* John Wiley, New York, 1986.

NEGOTIATING

Bacharach, Samuel B., and Lawler, Edward J. *Bargaining: Power Tactics and Outcomes.* Jossey-Bass, San Francisco, 1981.

Cohen, Herb. *You Can Negotiate Anything.* Bantam Press, New York, 1983.

Comiskey, James C. *Negotiating the Purchase or Sale of a Business.* PSI Research, Milpitas, CA, 1986.

Fisher, Roger, and William Ury. *Getting to Yes: Negotiating Agreement Without Giving In.* Houghton Mifflin, Boston, 1983.

Nierenberg, Gerald. *Fundamentals of Negotiating.* Harper & Row, New York, 1987.

Raffia, Howard. *The Art and Science of Negotiating.* The Belknap Press of Harvard University Press, Cambridge, MA, 1982.

NEWSPAPERS AND MAGAZINES

Business and Acquisition Newsletter. Newsletters International, Houston, monthly.

Business Opportunities Digest. Clarksville, TN, monthly.

Business Opportunities Journal. San Diego, CA, monthly.

Entrepreneur Magazine. American Entrepreneur's Association, Los Angeles, monthly.

Finders International. Hawley, PA, quarterly.

Inc., The Magazine for Growing Companies. Boston, monthly.

Mergers and Acquisitions. MLR Enterprises, Inc., Philadelphia, bimonthly.

The National Digest of Business Opportunities. Holmes, PA, weekly.

The Opportunity Market. Sarasota, FL.

Success Magazine. New York, monthly.

OTHER BOOKS

Baron, Paul B. *When You Buy or Sell a Company*. Center for Business Information, Meriden, CT, 1983.

Curtin, Richard. *Running Your Own Show: Mastering the Basics of Small Business*. New American Library, New York, 1983.

Cushman, Robert F. *Business Insurance Handbook*. Dow Jones-Irwin, Inc. Homewood, IL, 1981.

Franchise Annual: Handbook and Directory. Info Press, Lewiston, NY, annual.

Franchise Opportunities Handbook. Office of Consumer Goods and Service Industries, U.S. Dept. of Commerce, U.S. Government Printing Office, Washington, D.C., 20402.

Greve, J. Terrence. *How to Do a Leveraged Buyout*, 3rd ed. Business Publications, Inc., Homewood, IL, 1987.

Lasser (J. K.) Tax Institute. *How to Own a Small Business*. McGraw-Hill, New York, 1985.

Mandell, Donnan, ed. *The Dealmaker's Dictionary*. Business Publications, Inc., Homewood, IL, 1983.

Mason, L. Ryder, ed. *Structuring and Financing Management Buyouts*. Business Publications, Inc., Homewood, IL, 1983.

Small, Samuel, and Pilot Books Staff. *Directory of Franchising Organizations*. Pilot Books, New York, 1986.

The Small Business Reporter. Bank of America, Dept. 3120, San Francisco (a series of short books):

Guide to Tax Reform	*Management Transitions*
Business Computers from A to Z	*Business Financing*
How to Buy and Sell a Business	*Understanding Financial Statements*
or Franchise	*Financial Records for Small Business*
Marketing Small Business	*Personnel Guidelines*
Cash Flow/Cash Management	*Equipment Leasing*
Avoiding Management Pitfalls	*Crime Prevention for Small Business*

Smith, Brian R., and Thomas L. West. *Buying Your Own Small Business*. The Stephen Greene Press, Lexington, MA, 1985.

Tetreault, Wilfred E. *Buying and Selling Business Opportunities*. Addison-Wesley, Reading, MA, 1981.

RETIREMENT

Corrick, Frank. *Preparing for Your Retirement Years*. Pilot Books, New York, 1979.

Fromme, Allan. *Life After Work: Planning It, Living It, Loving It*. American Association of Retired Persons, Washington, D.C., 1984.

Miller, Herbert A. Jr. *Retirement Plans: An Information Sourcebook*. Oryx Press, Phoenix, AZ, 1987.

TAXES AND ESTATE PLANNING

Amling, Frederick, & Droms, William C. *Personal Financial Management*, 2nd ed. Irwin, New York, 1986.

Boone, Louis E., and Kurtz, David. *Contemporary Personal Finance*. Random House, New York, 1985.

Brod, Alice F. *Estate Planning: Complete Guide and Workbook*. Panel Publications, Greenvale, NY, 1984.

The Closely Held Business 1987, vol. 174. Tax Law & Estate Planning, Practicing Law Institute, New York.

Esperti, R. A., and Peterson, R. L. *The Handbook of Estate Planning*. McGraw-Hill, New York, 1987.

Estate Planning for Interests in a Closely Held Business. American Law Institute, Philadelphia, 1981 and Rev.

Hallman, G. Victor, and Rosenbloom, Jerry S. *Personal Financial Planning*. McGraw-Hill, New York, 1987.

Hamline University, Advanced Legal Education Staff. *Estate Planning for Owners of Small Businesses*. Hamline University School of Law, St. Paul, MN, 1986.

Hood, Edwin T., et al. *Closely Held Corporations in Business & Estate Planning*. Little, Brown, & Co., Boston, 1985.

Morse, David. *Retire Rich: Planning a Secure Financial Future*. Franklin Watts, Inc., New York, 1987.

Nauheim, Ferd. *The Retirement Money Book: Ways to Have More Income When You Retire*. Acropolis Books, Washington, D.C., 1982.

Ness, Theodore. *Tax Planning for the Disposition of Business Interests*. Warren, Gorman & Lamont, 1985.

Rothenberg, Waldo G. *Tax and Estate Planning with Closely Held Corporations*. Lawyers Cooperative, Rochester, NY, 1987.

Index